Walden; or, Life in the Woods

by Henry David Thoreau

A Study Guide by Ray Moore

Photograph of Henry David Thoreau, essayist and naturalist by Benjamin D. Maxham, 18th June, 1856. This image is in the public domain and is not subject to copyright. (Source: Wikimedia Commons)

Acknowledgements:
As always, I am indebted to the work of numerous editors and critics as I have acknowledged in the text and the Bibliography. Once again, I stand on the shoulders of giants. Where I am conscious of having taken an idea or a phrase from a particular author, I have cited the source in the text. Any failure to do so is an omission which I will immediately correct if it is drawn to my attention.

I believe that all quotations used in the book are either out of copyright (in the case of Thoreau) or fall under the definition of 'fair use'. Once again, if I am in error on any quotation, I will immediately correct if it is drawn to my attention.

Thanks are due to my wife, Barbara, for reading the manuscript, offering valuable suggestions, and putting the text into the correct formats for publication. Any errors which remain are my own.

Contents

Preface.. 1

Introduction: 2

Introduction to Transcendentalism 4

  Ralph Waldo Emerson (1803-1882).. 5

Introduction to *Walden*.. 6

Genre.. 7

Dramatis Personæ: A Selective List of Significant Characters 8

Narrative Voice.. 13

Themes 15

Walden; or, Life in the Woods 20

  Chapter One: Economy 20

  Chapter Two: Where I lived, and What I lived For 36

  Chapter Three: Reading.. 40

  Chapter Four: Sounds 42

  Chapter Five: Solitude.. 45

  Chapter Six: Visitors 47

  Chapter Seven: The Bean-Field 51

  Chapter Eight: The Ponds 54

  Chapter Nine: Baker Farm.. 58

  Chapter Ten: Higher Laws.. 60

  Chapter Eleven: Brute Neighbors... 63

  Chapter Twelve: House-Warming... 65

  Chapter Thirteen: Former Inhabitants; and Winter Visitors 69

  Chapter Fourteen: Winter Animals 72

  Chapter Fifteen: The Pond in Winter 73

  Chapter Sixteen: Spring.. 77

  Chapter Seventeen: Conclusion 81

  Post-reading Questions and Activities:... 83

Works Cited / Selected Bibliography:..83

Appendix 1: Literary Terms 84

Appendix 2: Classroom Use of the Study Guide Questions..............................87

To the Reader 89

Walden by Henry David Thoreau

Preface

A Study Guide is an *aid* to the close reading of a text; it is *never a substitute* for the close reading of a text. This classic text deserves to be read reflectively.

There is no disguising the fact that, in places, the language and expression in *Walden* can be difficult for the contemporary reader, particularly one coming to it for the first time. Thoreau's essential points do sometimes get lost in the detail and rhetoric of his expression. Being himself very well read in classical literature (and able to read it in the original Greek or Latin), Thoreau's writing in liberally sprinkled with literary allusions and references. Unless the reader is using an annotated edition of the text, most of these obscurities will sail well over his/her head and may be safely allowed to do so without any danger of the reader losing sight of the essential point being made.

The summaries and commentaries provided in this guide will allow students to get an *overview* of each chapter which will make reading what Thoreau wrote both easier and more productive. What makes this guide unique is that in the summaries I have relied, as far as possible, on quotation so that Thoreau can speak for himself. However, by their very nature, summaries miss out a great deal, and they are certainly *no substitute* for reading the text itself. Likewise, the commentaries provide a *starting point* for the reader's own reflections on each section/chapter. The analysis they provide represents my current understanding of the text. I have enough respect for my readers to assume that they will take what they find convincing and reject, or adapt, what they find unconvincing. My aim is to stimulate the reader *to develop his/her own understanding* of a text which profoundly touches the lives of those who make the effort to understand it.

Since *Walden* exists in so many different editions, I have not given page numbers for quotations. Because of the importance and meaning that Thoreau attached to the word, I have chosen to capitalize 'Nature' throughout *my* text. This is a personal decision.

Introduction:

Summary:

Henry David Thoreau's classic account of the two years he spent in a cabin of his own making near the shore of Walden Pond examines how we should live our lives. Thoreau's point is that most people do not actually *live* at all – they exist; they sleep-walk through life. Working hard to earn money for material possessions (i.e., 'stuff'), we fill up our time and expend our energy so that we have nothing of either left to contemplate our place in Nature, to become 'mindful' of our existence, or to develop our spirituality.

Thus, as well as being a bitter (and often very funny) satire of the society of his day (a satire which is, if anything, even more relevant to our own society), *Walden* is one of the first 'self-help' books and Thoreau one of the first 'life-coaches'. It is not that Thoreau wants every one of his readers to go and live alone in the forest; he is simply challenging each of us to get our priorities right, to clear the inessential clutter out of our lives, and "to live deliberately ... to front only the essential facts of life ... to live deep and suck out all the marrow of life ..."

After two years on Walden Pond, Thoreau reports that he moved out of his little cabin because he wanted to experience the world from a different perspective.

Why Read this Book?

Most students will read this book because it is required by their syllabus, but in doing so they may just make the acquaintance of a teacher who will wake them up and remind them of the difference between 'going through the motions' and actually living.

Speaking to his son George about taking away some of his books because he is moving house, Mr. Emerson says, "You can take all those, but leave me Thoreau till I go. I need him by me now" (*A Room with a View* by E. M. Forster). The sensitive reader might, in years to come, develop the same affection for and reliance on Thoreau's voice of sanity in an increasingly manic world.

Important: Issues with this Book.

The main issue that readers find with this book is that the prose can be dense and the argument convoluted, not entirely consistent, and therefore hard to follow. "It cannot, I think, be denied that Walden sometimes seems an enormously long and boring book," writes Cavell near the beginning of his study of the book (20). The main justification for this Study Guide is that it aims to make the text accessible, to rescue the key ideas from the ornate prose in which Thoreau (like his great friend Ralph Waldo Emerson) tended to wrap them.

There are many studies of *Walden* available to the reader/student. I have found, however, that most tend to mystify the text rather than to clarify its meaning, and that those which do set out to clarify end up either paraphrasing the obvious or (much worse) misrepresenting what Thoreau says. My aim in this Guide has been to show the relevance and to capture the excitement of Thoreau's ideas. I leave it to the reader to evaluate my success.

Introduction to Transcendentalism

> Emerson had said, "There is no pure Transcendentalist"; Thoreau
> wished to see what pure transcendentalism was, and went to Walden.
> (Van Doren 71-2)

If you know anything about Henry David Thoreau (1817-1842), it is probably that he was a Transcendentalist, which is a very long and slightly intimidating word. What did it mean? In one sentence, it meant that "For Thoreau nature was the path to the divine, not an end in itself" (Sullivan 218).

Whole books have been written on the origin and evolution of Transcendentalism, so what follows is necessarily a simplification. Transcendentalism was an American intellectual and religious movement begun in the 1820s in the area around Boston, Massachusetts. It was a protest against the prevailing Unitarian ministry and faith. Put simply, Transcendentalism rejected the concept of an anthropomorphic god (the old man in the sky with a long beard painted on the ceiling of the Sistine Chapel by Michelangelo between 1508 and 1512) and of divine texts (such as the Bible or the Koran) which claim authoritatively to convey the will of such a god. Transcendentalism rejected the idea that man can only learn about God at second hand (by reading the Bible, listening to sermons and observing in Nature, God's creation) for the conviction that *man can directly experience the divine.*

Ralph Waldo Emerson, one of the acknowledged leaders of this movement held that each person must find his or her "original relation to the universe" in solitude amidst Nature. For the Transcendentalist, "nature, including human beings, has the power and authority traditionally attributed to an independent deity" (*Stanford Encyclopedia of Philosophy*). So 'god' is the creator of Nature, and every part of Nature, including man, is *part* of the Creator. In his essay *Nature* (1836), Emerson writes: "[Nature] always speaks of Spirit. It suggests the Absolute ... the noblest ministry of nature, is to stand as the apparition of God." Man is a part of Nature, and a universal essence is present in each and every object, including humans. Nature is "a projection of God in the unconscious ..." (Transcendentalism was heavily influenced by Romanticism and Indian philosophy).

Since Nature, humanity, and God are *one*, then the transcendent God is present in every physical aspect of Nature, and so the way for human beings to experience their own unity with God is to become aware of their place in Nature. This is why *Walden* continually demonstrates 'correspondences' between the ethical and intellectual life of humans and what Thoreau observes in Nature: the patterns discernible in Natural phenomena are replicated in humans.

Emerson outlined his views in "The Divinity School Address" delivered at Harvard on July 15, 1838. However, while Emerson saw in Nature a *symbol* of the spiritual, Thoreau, at least in *Walden*, went much further and seemed to *equate* Nature with God and the *experience* of Nature with *experience* of the divine. For Thoreau, immersion in Walden Pond was a form of baptism. Little wonder, then, that the book was attacked for preaching pantheism ("a doctrine that equates God with the forces and laws of the universe" Merriam-Webster).

Ralph Waldo Emerson (1803-1882)

In his influential essay "The American Scholar" (1837) Emerson defines three stages in the development of the transcendentalist: first, establish a harmonious relationship with Nature; second, study the writings of the past; and third, apply what has been learned to reforming and improving society. Emerson argues that Nature is the first influence upon the human mind both in time and in importance. As man begins to classify the things he finds in Nature, he comes to understand that "these objects are not chaotic, and not foreign, but have a law which is also the law of the human mind ... Its beauty is the beauty of his own mind." Thus, the more knowledge man has of Nature, the greater is his understanding of the self; the greater is his understanding of the self, the more knowledge man has of Nature.

Books are our means of access to the great minds of the past, but books are not perfect. Though in books writers transform "short-lived actions" into "immortal thoughts," every book contains only partial truth since it is a product of the time in which it was written. Each age must write its own books for the next succeeding generation, "The books of an older period will not fit this." Thus, readers make an error if they, young men in libraries, study books reverently, forget that these books were originally written by young men in libraries (Cicero, Locke, Bacon, etc.). Excessive reading of books diverts the scholar from original thought expressed in the scholar's *own words.*

The right use of books is to inspire. "Man Thinking [*sic.*] must not be subdued by his instruments ... When he can read God directly [in Nature], the hour is too precious to be wasted in other men's transcripts of their reading" (55). When reading is done, it must be "creative" reading not merely receptive reading. Certainly the college student must read, sometimes laboriously, to amass knowledge, but education must never forget the creative spirit.

Since the world is an expression of ourselves, action in the world is essential to a thinking person: "Action is with the scholar subordinate, but it is essential ... The true scholar grudges every opportunity of action passed by, as a loss of power. It is the raw material out of which the intellect moulds her splendid products ... he who has put forth his total strength in fit actions, has the riches return of wisdom."

The reader of *Walden* will recognize much of Emerson's thinking. *Walden* is Thoreau's attempt at taking action by making a difference to the quality of life of his fellow man.

Introduction to *Walden*

> If Emerson *studied* Nature to know himself, Thoreau *wedded* Nature
> to know himself. (Van Doren 28, emphasis added)

There are certain common misconceptions about Thoreau's decision to go to the woods. He was neither a hermit (though he sometimes refers to himself as such), a frontiersman, nor a lazy loafer (though his neighbors often called him that), and he did *not* go off to live in the wilds. He built his cabin on a previously occupied spot about twenty minutes walk from the town of Concord, Massachusetts. He did *not* cut himself off from society: he welcomed visitors to his cabin and walked to Concord nearly every day, often calling into the home of his great friend Ralph Waldo Emerson for a meal (though this fact is absent from *Walden*). He was *not* entirely self-sufficient: for one thing, he did not own the land on which he built his cabin (Emerson did), and for another, he made money doing odd jobs for people as he did pretty much all of his life. He was *not* a strict vegetarian, though he probably thought he should have been. He was *not*, as some of his contemporaries in Concord believed, a loafer: during his time at Walden Pond, he did jobs for others, tended his own garden, and wrote a great deal.

Here are the facts. From July 4th, 1845 (Independence Day!), until September 6th, 1847, Thoreau (then in his late twenties) lived one and a half miles outside of Concord, in a one-room cabin of his own construction adjacent to Walden Pond. He was there exactly two years, two months and two days. The first mention of living such a life occurs in his *Journal* for 1841, "I want to go soon and live away by the pond ...Will it not be employment enough to watch the progress of the seasons?" The immediate motive for moving out of the family home in town was that Thoreau needed somewhere quieter than the family boarding house (run by his mother) or the adjacent pencil factory (managed by his father) to work on writing the book *A Week on the Concord and Merrimack Rivers* (published 1849). More fundamentally, he went in order to "conduct an experiment in economic independence," to see if there was a viable alternative to the life he saw all around him, a life spent in almost constant work to the exclusion of time for "intellectual and spiritual labor" (Schneider in Myerson ed. 93). [At other times in his life, Thoreau *did* work in the pencil factory that his father managed and his research into German pencil-making techniques significantly improved the end product which had the reputation of being the best quality pencil manufactured in the United States.]

For most of his adult life, Thoreau kept a daily Journal, and just as he used that Journal as source material for *A Week*, so *Walden* was "made up out of as many as sixteen years of the Journal (1838-54)" (Van Doren 75-6). Given that the book was first published (with the title *Walden, or Life in the Woods* by the Boston firm of Ticknor and Fields) on August 9, 1854, just over seven years after

Thoreau left the Pond, it is clear that he put significant time and effort into its composition. This was rewarded by positive reviews and reasonably strong sales.

Genre

Walden is not fiction, because it is based upon something that the author actually did, but it is not autobiography either because it is not a chronological account of what the author did. (Thoreau condenses the two years he spent on the pond into a single year the better to reflect the passage of the four seasons). Neither is the author the center of interest. In fact, it is impossible to identify *Walden* with a single genre. The book is a combination of spiritual autobiography, critique of social values, satire, philosophical thesis, nature journal, essay and self-help manual. (Even then, I have probably missed something.) In structure, it is basically chronological, tracing the cycle of the seasons as through the fruitfulness of early summer and autumn to the symbolic death represented by a harsh winter and the rebirth of life symbolized by spring.

Perhaps the text is best defined as a work of practical philosophy, a guide book to beginning the journey inward, for to Thoreau his two years on Walden Pond were intended simply as a preparation for further explorations of the full potentialities of living.

Dramatis Personæ: A Selective List of Significant Characters

The people who either appear in the events of the narrative or are simply referred to in passing are either real, historical figures (though their names are seldom used) or representative stereotypes. They are not really fictional characters such as would appear in a novel since, with the exception of Thoreau, none is developed in depth: they are, as it were, figures in a landscape.

Historical figures in and around Concord:

Henry David Thoreau – The narrator of *Walden* is identifiably the historical naturalist, essayist, and poet who was a protégé of the great American philosopher and essayist Ralph Waldo Emerson (1803-1882) on whose land he built a cabin adjacent to Walden Pond. It would be an error, however, to equate the narrative voice with the historical Thoreau. The narrator is a comic creation: the 'Crank of Concord', or, if you prefer, the 'Curmudgeon of Concord' (Sullivan). This man exaggerates, makes fun of his neighbors and/or of himself, and is inconsistent and often irritating. The narrative voice adopted by the author aims

to make the reader question what he/she values in life.

Thoreau divides this self into two entities:

> ***The Hermit***, who just wants to sit and philosophize (he is a student on Confucius whom he calls "Con-fut-see), and represents man's spiritual nature.

> ***The Poet***, who wants to look at the sky and go fishing, and represents the animal nature in man, being interested in the material aspects of life – he represents man's physical nature.

John Thoreau – Elder brother to Thoreau for whom he had great respect. In 1842, John accidentally cut himself with a razor. The small wound went untreated; he developed lockjaw, and eventually died in Thoreau's arms. Thoreau was profoundly affected by his brother's death.

Ralph Waldo Emerson – The essayist and poet was the leading figure of American Transcendentalism. Emerson became a mentor to Thoreau after they met in 1837. Despite revealing to the reader that he built his cabin on land owned by another person, the narrator fails to mention Emerson's name. When Emerson visits, he is called "Old Immortal" and described respectfully almost as the narrator's guru.

Lidian Emerson – Emerson's second wife and a close friend of Thoreau.

Neighbors:

James Collins – Collins, an Irishman who works for the Fitchburg Railroad, is moving away with his wife and family, so Thoreau purchases his cabin (for $4.25) and reuses the boards to build his own shelter at Walden.

Walden by Henry David Thoreau

Seeley – An Irish neighbor of the Collins', he steals the reusable staples, nails, and spikes from the Collins' boards before Thoreau carts the wood to Walden.

The Owner of the Hollowell Farm – Thoreau agrees to buy this unnamed man's farm and gives him $10 as deposit. Then the man's wife changes her mind about selling the farm. Greatly relieved, Thoreau lets him keep the $10 considering that he is still better off because he has avoided the burden of ownership.

Mr. Gilian Baker – Baker lives with his wife in Lincoln, about two miles south of Concord Battlefield.
He is rumored to be the owner of a fantastic 'winged cat.' Thoreau makes a special visit to see this wonder, but the cat is nowhere to be seen. Mr. Baker gives Thoreau a pair of the cat's 'wings' which turn out to be long, matted flaps of fur.

The Woodchopper – He is an unnamed Canadian laborer [identified by critics as Alex Thérien] in his late twenties, who has been living in the States for twelve years, hoping to earn the money to buy a farm in Canada. Thoreau admires him for his skill with an axe and regards him as a "natural man" in whom "the animal man chiefly was developed." He had been taught to read and write, but the priests who educated him never awakened his consciousness. As a result, he does not really understand the words he decodes, nor is he capable of using writing to express own thoughts. Intellectually and spiritually, Thoreau considers him a child.

Ice-cutters – These men come in January to cut the ice of Walden Pond and cart it away. They are Irish laborers with Yankee overseers, working for a man who already has $500,000. Walden freezes over again and when the ice blocks left behind as unusable melt, they drain back into the pond.

Those who visited Thoreau:

A Long-headed farmer – One of Thoreau's winter visitors, this man walks through the snowy woods to his cabin to "have a social crack [i.e., gossip]." Thoreau talks with him of the past times.

The Poet – An unnamed friend stays with Thoreau for a week and helps him with the building of his chimney. He appears at other times, being one of Thoreau's few winter visitors, coming the farthest and through the worst weather. He is always practical and living in the real world. Thoreau values his company and conversation, but the two are very different. (This unnamed character has been identified by most critics as William Ellery Channing, a Minister and Thoreau's closest friend. Channing was an organizer of groups [in which he differed fundamentally from Thoreau] that opposed slavery, war, and drunkenness [causes in which Thoreau and Channing were united].)

The Philosopher – He is a visitor during the winter evenings of Thoreau's second winter on the Pond. Their long philosophical talks reveal the man's faith in humanity which is much greater than is Thoreau's. [This character has been identified by most critics as Amos Bronson Alcott, a fellow Transcendentalist who was active in education and communal living projects. He was the father of Louisa May Alcott author of *Little Women*.]

The Old Hunter – This man bathes in Walden Pond once every summer and visits Thoreau.

Runaway Slave – This man arrives at Walden Pond on route to Canada using the 'Underground Railway'. Thoreau helps him "toward the n'rthstar."

Former residents of Walden now deceased:

An Old Settler – The spirit of this long-dead man visits Thoreau in the evenings. He was the original owner and the man who is reputed "to have dug Walden Pond, and stoned it, and fringed it with pine woods." To Thoreau, he represents the creative force or spirit of the place.

An Elderly Dame – The only evidence of this spiritual entity is the "odorous herb garden" through which Thoreau loves to stroll "gathering simples [medicinal herbs] and listening to her fables." Her spirit represents the female aspect of the creative force, the essence of Nature that is always alive and health-giving.

Cato Ingraham – This long-dead, former inhabitant who occupied a house east of Thoreau's cabin had been the slave of Duncan Ingraham, Esq. a Concord lawyer. Ingraham built his slave a house and gave him permission to live in the woods. All that is left of Cato's house is its overgrown cellar. The patch of walnuts he planted near his house for convenience in his old age was harvested by a whiter speculator.

Zilpha Ingraham - This black woman had a house where the corner of Thoreau's field is located. She spun linen for the townspeople and sang while doing so. British war prisoners on parole during the War of 1812 burned down her house, with her dog, cat, and chickens inside. Thoreau has seen bricks amid the oaks where it once stood.

Brister Freeman – He was the former slave of Squire Cummings and his house was on Brister's Hill, where the apple trees he planted still bear fruit. He fought and died in the battle of Lexington and Concord. His gravestone, in the Lincoln cemetery, where he is buried near the unmarked graves of British soldiers killed in the Revolution, reads 'Sippio Brister', though Thoreau compares him to Roman general Scipio Africanus, "a man of color." His wife, **Fenda**, Thoreau remembers as benevolently telling fortunes.

Stratten –A family whose homestead was near Brister's Hill. Their orchard once covered the hill but is now overgrown by pitch pines.

Walden by Henry David Thoreau

Breed – The name of a family whose house and tavern stood at the edge of the woods. The house stood empty for a dozen years until some boys from the village mischievously lit it on fire one election night. Thoreau was one of the crowd who ran to fight the fire, but it was decided to let the house burn. The next day, Thoreau encountered the only remaining member of the Breed family, who had come to look at the old house and found it burned to the ground.

Wyman – A potter who squatted with his family in the woods near the pond, he never paid any taxes despite the sheriff's attempts to collect them. He sold his goods in Concord. When a man who bought the potter's wheel from Wyman's son inquired of his whereabouts, Thoreau was glad to hear that such an ancient art had been practiced in his neighborhood.

Hugh Quoil – An well-mannered Irishman, called 'Colonel Quoil', who was rumored to have been at the Battle of Waterloo, lived in Wyman's house after Wyman passed away and worked as a ditcher. He suffered badly with a trembling delirium and was found dead in the road soon after Thoreau moved to Walden and so he did not know him well, though he did visit the man's house although some of his neighbors worried it was unlucky to do so.

Sam Nutting – He is a hunter who used to hunt bears in Concord in exchange for rum. Bears are no longer seen around Walden.

Representative stereotypes:

John Field – The name suggests that he is a composite figure typical of many of the poor working men whom Thoreau knew. He is a poor Irish-American laborer who lives with his wife and many children in a refurbished cabin on the Baker Farm just outside of Concord. He is a "bogger" working at digging up meadows and bogs for farmers so that they can plough and plant the land. Thoreau treats him with condescension as one who works hard but never prospers because he spends his income on consumer goods that Thoreau is convinced he does not need. The materialism which brought him from Ireland is, paradoxically, keeping him financially and spiritually poor. Thoreau tries to convert Field and his wife to his own simpler existence, but they are unmoved by his arguments.

Mrs. Field – She is treated as dismissively as her husband. Her constant efforts to keep the cabin clean appear to achieve no results.

John Farmer – Sitting in his doorway one September evening, thinking about the work of the day, his thoughts are interrupted by the sound of Thoreau's flute, which suggests the possibility of a higher mode of existence. (The imagined scene is a metaphor for the effect Thoreau hopes his book will have on his readers.)

John Smith – As he imagines where the hogsheads of molasses or brandy on the passing railroad are headed, Thoreau invents this trader from Cuttingsville, Vermont.

National and international figures:

Henry Clay – To Thoreau, the politician Clay (1777-1852) was "the Great Compromiser" for his role in the Missouri Compromise and the Compromise of 1850. Thoreau, a fierce opponent of slavery, was a staunch critic of Clay.

James Russell Lowell – Lowell (1819-1891) was the author of the poetic satire *The Bigelow Papers*, professor of modern languages at Harvard, and an editor and diplomat.

Confucius – Confucius (551-479 B.C.) was a Chinese teacher, editor, politician, and philosopher known for his sayings and parables which were collected under the title *Analects*. He was one of Thoreau's favorite authors.

Mencius – Mencius (372-289 B.C.) was a Chinese philosopher and disciple of Confucius. He was best known for his anthology of sayings and stories collected under the title *The Book of Mencius*.

Walden by Henry David Thoreau

Narrative Voice

> If 'Walden' is the best transcendental book, that is partly because it is written in bounding spirits, with eyes twinkling and tongue in cheek. (Van Doren 11)

Walden dispenses with the convention of the third person omniscient [all-knowing] narrator. Thoreau begins with a justification for his decision to break with literary convention by addressing himself directly to his reader in the first person singular voice: "In most books, the *I*, or first person, is omitted; in this it will be retained; that, in respect to egotism, is the main difference. We commonly do not remember that it is, after all, always the first person that is speaking." The true focus of the book is on the developing consciousness of the narrator, the spiritual growth of his self, or soul, as he conducts his experiment in the simplification of life. Thoreau, however, frequently switches to first person plural ("We don garment after garment...") because he knows himself to be part of the society whose values he criticizes, and to the second-person point of view ("Could you, in such a case, tell ...") to address the reader directly because Thoreau is above all a teacher.

Ken Kifer identifies three reasons why *Walden* is a difficult book for the modern reader:

- It was written in the rhetorically dense prose of its period. Kifer lists: "extended, allegorical metaphors, long and complex paragraphs and sentences, and vivid, detailed, and insightful descriptions ... metaphors, allusions, understatement, hyperbole, personification, irony, satire, metonymy, synecdoche, and oxymorons," in addition to Thoreau's tendency to "shift from a scientific to a transcendental point of view in mid-sentence." To this, we may add Thoreau's frequent use of anaphora. [Readers should be reassured that understanding, identifying and analyzing Thoreau's use of rhetorical devices is not necessary to understand his message. A list of Literary Terms is included as Appendix 1.]

- The entire argument of the book is based on an understanding of life that is "quite contrary to what most people would call common sense" – in a nut-shell, the paradoxical idea that 'less is more'. Kifer adds that Thoreau's logic "is based on what most people say they believe" but do not actually believe. No one is going to *admit* that they believe the only thing worth having in life is material possessions; everyone is going to *claim* that it is the experience of life itself that they value. Recognizing the basic dishonesty of society and of his readers, Thoreau "fills *Walden* with sarcasm, paradoxes, and double entendres"; he takes delight in teasing, challenging, and fooling his readers.

- What Thoreau is trying to communicate is an intuition, a state of being, which "any words would be inadequate at expressing."
(Kifer's comments are quoted in full in the Wikipedia article on *Walden*.)

As narrator, Thoreau is a harsh critic of the form of life that he rejects and which was/is the life of most of his readers. Schneider calls his tone "sternly didactic and judgmental" (Myerson Ed. 98). Perhaps fortunately, the narrator is saved from the charge of being sanctimonious [i.e., assuming a position of moral superiority] by his ready wit and his sense of humor, both of which he is as likely to turn against himself as he is to use to criticize his fellow man. The comic aspect of Walden has been so frequently overlooked or minimized that I was particularly pleased to read the following:

> Walden is a work intended to revive America, a communal work that is forever pigeonholed as a reclusive one. And what is perhaps most surprising is that it's *a comedy*; it's *an economic satire* draped in the language of nature and farming and the self-help books of the day that shows the mass of economic men to be a bunch of unwitting saps ... Thoreau is *a humorist* with the eye of *a social satirist*, who, when he read aloud from his work-in-progress on the trips he did take out of town, often had his audiences in *complete hysterics* - as Emerson once described it in his journal, 'They laughed till they cried'... [He] was *joking* to prod, punning to motivate, to inspire, to reform, in a world that he had a difficult time in but that nevertheless inspired him. (Sullivan 7, 14, 15, emphasis added)

Walden by Henry David Thoreau

Themes

> Nature expected nothing of him … His ideal was independence; Nature never criticized him. His ideal demanded something absolutely to be trusted, capable of any interpretation, inexhaustible to any curious mind, giving all and taking nothing, yet not complaining of the sacrifice; Nature was all that. (Van Doren 35)

One of the reasons that *Walden* is not an easy book to follow, particularly for the first-time reader, is that the ideas that Thoreau expresses contain many contradictions. This is not a book which presents its ideas in a clear and logical progression towards a simple conclusion; it is a work that presents the process of forming ideas. As a result, there are many gaps, discontinuities, extravagant generalizations, paradoxes, and inconsistencies. This is deliberate: it is not Thoreau's aim to provide the reader with solutions but to stimulate the reader into asking questions. This is a book that denies the existence of an objective truth on which all right-thinking people must agree; rather, it urges every reader to put down *Walden* and find for him/herself the essential meaning of existence.

It is particularly difficult to separate out the themes of this book since they are all so interconnected. To avoid repetition, I have kept each theme brief.

Living life to the full:

Thoreau is convinced that the mass of people sleepwalk their way through life willfully ignorant of life's true importance and potential. Most people are so busy making a living that they have no time or energy to actually live. *Walden* is an account of the process by which the Thoreau purified his life and attained spiritual fulfillment. It is a joyous celebration of life and a call for all men to realize the full potential of life. It is a practical guide to spirituality, a recreation of the heightened consciousness that Thoreau achieved for himself, and a call for readers to find their own path to spiritual fulfillment.

Self-discovery and the search for enlightenment:

> To magnify the self, to have sensations of infinitude, to thrum [i.e., make a continuous rhythmic humming sound] with the excitement of the universe, was the ambition of the man who went to Walden Pond. (Van Doren 112)

The spiritual core of *Walden* is the belief that man is a part of Nature. Thoreau believed that through a close relationship with Nature, people could perfect themselves by following the inner light of consciousness. To Thoreau, life was a tremendous gift that most people appeared not to appreciate. He believed spiritual reality was embedded in the physical reality of Nature (rather than, say, in the holy texts of various religions). Purifying the self from the false values of society and developing an understanding of man's place in eternal Nature was for Thoreau the way to the enlightenment spoken of by mystics

15

throughout human history. In his *Journals* he wrote, "I love nature, because it never cheats me. It never jests. It is cheerfully, musically earnest."

Self-reliance:

> Life is an art. When we consider what life may be to all, and what it is to most, we shall see how little this art is yet understood ... the work of life, so far as the individual is concerned, ... is self-culture, – the perfect unfolding of our individual nature ... The business of self-culture admits of no compromise ... All that is best in human attainment springs from retirement ... In retirement, we first become acquainted with ourselves, our means, and ends. ("The Art of Life – The Scholar's Calling" by Frederick Henry Hedge, *Dial*, 1840)

In going to the woods, Thoreau aimed, as far as possible, to live an economically self-sufficient life. This meant spending as little money as possible and only money he had earned by his own labor. Practically speaking, he borrowed, scavenged, re-cycled, ate mainly the food he could raise himself or catch, and did casual labor when he needed the money. The aim of this economic independence was to limit the amount of time spent each day in working and to maximize the amount of time available to experience *being alive*. To Thoreau, this spiritual quest was essentially solitary, and so (although he certainly did not cut himself off from people) he was also emotionally self-reliant.

Simplifying life:

Thoreau lived at a time when the (relatively new) factory system was producing consumer goods on a scale unprecedented in history. Producers found a ready market for their goods, and where there was no market they increasingly used advertising to stimulate one. The result, in Thoreau's mind, was a vicious circle: people work longer hours to get more money to buy 'stuff' that they think they need, and still longer hours to get more and better 'stuff' – a vicious circle. In contrast, *Walden* says that living simply liberates you from your obsession with material possessions and frees up your time for the things that *really count* in life – what we today would call 'quality time'. To Thoreau this meant reading, writing, thinking and experiencing Nature rather than working so be able to afford inessential 'luxuries'.

Love and respect for Nature:

Aside from the spiritual aspect of Thoreau's relationship with Nature, he was a person who simply enjoyed being outside (in almost all weathers) rather than inside and who lamented the way in which the expansion of settlement and the development of intensive agriculture was destroying the beauty of the natural world. He could literally see this process in the area around Concord by comparing the present with the much less developed, idyllic landscape that he remembered from his childhood there. The ice-cutters who descend on the Pond every winter to 'harvest' its ice to cool summer drinks in cities far away are the

most obvious symbols of this despoliation, along with those who strip the trees of berries to feed
the markets in towns. In this he is a proto-conservationist and forerunner of the Green movement.

The encroachment of technology:

Even on Walden Pond, Thoreau cannot escape the sound of the railway, the pollution of the steam engines, or the evidence of the trees felled to build the line. He is also aware of the media of communication (letters, the telegram, newspapers) but believes that very little of importance is ever communicated through them. In Thoreau's opinion, 'progress' is a myth: we are simply getting technologically advanced without advancing in intelligence. In contemporary terms, we might say that people are suffering from 'information overload' and are no longer able to distinguish the important from the trivial.

Opposition to government:

In so far as the government of the United States, at the time Thoreau wrote, supported slavery (at least in some states) and war (specifically the Mexican-American War, 1846-1848) as an instrument of an expansionist foreign policy (both of which Thoreau found morally repugnant) he stood in opposition to that government. He mentions, almost in passing, being placed in jail during a visit to Concord for failing to pay his poll taxes because of his conscientious objection to war. (After spending only the night in jail, Thoreau was released after an unknown woman paid his back taxes.) Above all, Thoreau is suspicious of patriotism: he calls it "the maggot in [the] heads" of the people (Conclusion). Thoreau would have agreed with the remark attributed to Samuel Johnson: "Patriotism is the last refuge of a scoundrel" (1775).

The vision of an ideal community:

It is not that Thoreau is against the concept of community but that he believes that communities have got their priorities all wrong. His ideal is a learning-community in which the highest priority is the continuing education of its citizens, and in which this aim is advanced by the spending of tax dollars.

Pre-Reading

Consider, and ideally discuss, the following questions:

1. What are the three biggest time-wasters in your life? How much control do you have over these things? Why do you allow them to waste so much of your time?

2. Imagine that you have got a free hour (no homework, no chores, no extra-curricular activities, yeah!). Explain how you would spend the hour. Justify spending the sixty minutes in this way.

3. Imagine that you were going to the family cabin in the woods for three weeks (of course, you may have first to imagine that your family has a cabin!)

Assuming that the cabin already has the basic essentials for survival (clothing, food, water and fuel), what are the five things that you would take with you? Justify each one. Arrange them in priority order.

4. What career do you have in mind? What would be the optimum number of hours a week you would want to work in this career? How do you envisage yourself spending your leisure time as an adult?

5. As an adult, which would be more important to you, earning enough to get by but not enough for luxuries, or earning enough to be able to buy luxury items?

WALDEN;

OR,

LIFE IN THE WOODS.

By HENRY D. THOREAU,

AUTHOR OF "A WEEK ON THE CONCORD AND MERRIMACK RIVERS."

I do not propose to write an ode to dejection, but to brag as lustily as chanticleer in the morning, standing on his roost, if only to wake my neighbors up. — Page 92.

BOSTON:

TICKNOR AND FIELDS.

M DCCC LIV.

Title page from first edition of Henry David Thoreau's *Walden* (1854)
(Image is in the public domain. Source: Wikimedia Commons.).

Walden; or, Life in the Woods

The questions are not designed to test you, but to help you to locate and to understand the settings, ideas and themes in the text. They do not normally have simple answers, nor is there always one answer. Consider a range of possibly interpretations – preferably by discussing the questions with others. Disagreement is to be encouraged!

Chapter One: Economy

"When I wrote ... on that basis."
Bottom line:

Having material possessions ('stuff') does not enrich the experience of living; it is a distraction from everything that is important and valuable in life. "One travels through life best by simplifying bodily needs to leave more time and energy for pursuing transcendental reality" (Schneider in Myerson Ed. 98).

Summary:

The argument (or thesis) is that men spend their time laboring on their farms and at their jobs leaving neither time nor energy to reflect on the nature and potential of their lives: "I see young men, my townsmen, whose misfortune it is to have inherited farms, houses, barns, cattle, and farming tools; for these are more easily acquired than got rid of."

Most men spend their lives, "trying to get into business and trying to get out of debt." This is a mistake that has grave consequences: "Most men, even in this comparatively free country, through mere ignorance and mistake, are so occupied with the factitious cares and superfluously coarse labors of life that its finer fruits cannot be plucked by them ... [T]he laboring man has not leisure for a true integrity day by day ... He has no time to be anything but a machine ... The mass of men lead lives of quiet desperation." Effectively, men have become slave-drivers *of themselves*. In contrast, Thoreau asserts that man is *free* to live differently but that a change in life-style must come from within: "What a man thinks of himself, that it is which determines, or rather indicates, his fate."

The fact that life appears always to have been as it is now is no recommendation for it: "No way of thinking or doing, however, ancient, can be trusted without proof ... Age is no better, hardly so well, qualified for an instructor as youth ... Practically, the old have no very important advice to give the young, their own experience has been so partial, and their lives have been such miserable failures." Uncritical adherence to traditional, to conventional ways of living as dictated by previous generations, is a barrier to personal growth; subversive, revolutionary ideas are required to set men free, and these the narrator intends to advocate.

The full potential of human consciousness has yet to be explored: "[M]an's capacities have never been measured; nor are we to judge of what he can do by any precedents, so little has been tried." Rather than spend our time building up a store of money and goods against some anticipated disaster in the future, we should live life with more confidence, live more in the moment: "I think that we may safely trust a good deal more than we do. ... The incessant anxiety and strain of some is a well-nigh incurable form of disease."

Commentary:

The book is addressed directly to the reader immediately establishing a personal relationship between writer and reader: "I would fain say something ... concerning ... you who read these pages ... something about your condition, especially your outward condition or circumstances in this world ... what it is, whether it is necessary that it be as bad as it is, whether it cannot be improved ..." Clearly the narrator regards himself as someone with something very important to say.

The primary focus of *Walden* will be on the spiritual rebirth and growth that Thoreau experienced during his time at Walden Pond. In the course of his argument, he will offer a critique of contemporary culture, of society, of economic theory and of politics, but these things follow from and are dependent upon Thoreau's vision of a better way to live. That vision came from the personal and subjective experience of spiritual fulfillment and religious ecstasy which he achieved through coming to understand man's place in Nature.

Thoreau intends to turn all accepted values on their head, so that, for example, a young man inheriting a farm is presented as a "misfortune," and the old are dismissed as having "no very important advice to give the young." He establishes the narrative voice as that of an unapologetic, consciously extremist contrarian. The pursuit of wealth and prestige, the work ethic that values labor of and for itself, the wisdom of our elders, and the conventional definitions of good behavior, are all called into question and implicitly or explicitly overturned. This is iconoclastic writing at its most extreme. The tone is, however, light. Thoreau is also very fond of puns (i.e., words which sound alike but have different meanings), paradoxes (i.e., statements that, on first reading, seem contradictory or absurd but, upon reflection, are found to be meaningful, valid or true), and the conscious use of clichés (i.e., overused and outworn phrases that suggest lack of original thought) for comic effect. It takes a very alert reader to pick up all of Thoreau's jokes, because few of us are as sensitized to language as he was. He has great fun pointing out the comic paradoxes that occur in what passes for conventional life: the coats for which we worked so long are eaten by moths in the closet, the free man becomes his own slave-driver, and the farmer who is convinced that vegetarianism cannot sustain his bones has his plough pulled by vegetarian cattle.

The statement, "The mass of men lead lives of quiet desperation," is central to Thoreau's thesis. He deliberately uses hyperbole in his choice of the word "desperation" rather than, say, 'dejection' or 'discontent'. Unlike these milder words, the concept of despair has religious connotations since it indicates a loss of faith. Adding the word "quiet" almost creates an oxymoron since we normally associate despair with wailing and lamentation. Thoreau believes that society's elevation of success and wealth as the only goals worth valuing leads men to the single-minded pursuit of money which ruins the lives of those who engage in it. The "desperation" of which he speaks is not only hidden from others but scarcely acknowledged (i.e., it is repressed) by those who suffer. Deep down, these men know that they are unable to appreciate the simpler pleasures described in *Walden*, but they also know that they are doomed to fail in their pursuit of material possessions. This is the great unspoken truth of modern society.

Thoreau preempts criticism that he is being arrogant and condescending. He makes no extravagant claims for his experiment in living, acknowledging that it *was* simply a short-term experiment and not a particularly adventurous one at that. (After all, at the time he lived in his cabin, real pioneers in the West were *actually living* at the edge of civilization.) He admits that he is now "a sojourner in civilized life again" and apologizes for being constricted to writing about himself "by the narrowness of my experience."

Questions:
1. The text is full of jokes, often at the narrator's own expense ("I should not talk so much about myself if there were any body else whom I knew so well"), and more often at the expense of his neighbors and potential readers (people like the opinionated farmer). Select just one more example of Thoreau's use of humor and comment on its purpose.
2. The narrator says that he is writing for those "who are said to live in New England." This is a deliberately ambiguous statement. What is Thoreau implying by the inclusion of the phrase "are said"?
3. Explain what the narrator means when he states that one cannot "kill time without injuring eternity."
4. "The greater part of what my neighbors call good I believe in my soul to be bad, and if I repent of anything, it is very likely to be my good behavior." Explain what Thoreau means by this paradoxical statement.

"Let us consider ... silver fetters"
Bottom line:
Thoreau set out "to learn what are the gross necessities of life and what methods have been taken to obtain them." In striving after things that cannot in any sense be said to be necessary to life, man places his entire being in chains by robbing himself of free time.

Summary:
Since man spends so much of his time working to secure the things that he believes to be necessary to

life, it seems reasonable to ask just what *is* essential to life: "The necessaries of life for man in this climate may, accurately enough, be distributed under the several heads of Food, Shelter, Clothing, and Fuel; for not till we have secured these are we prepared to entertain the true problems of life with freedom and a prospect of success … At the present day, and in this country, as I find by my own experience, a few implements, a knife, an axe, a spade, a wheelbarrow, etc., and for the studious, lamplight, stationery, and access to a few books, rank next to necessaries, and can all be obtained at a trifling cost."

Even with these 'essentials', men today tend to go to excess, buying more coats than they can wear and heating their rooms so hot that "they are cooked, of course *à la mode*." Man's body has its own "vital heat." When one goes beyond laboring to secure the essentials of life, one is laboring to secure the *inessentials*: "Most of the luxuries, and many of the so-called comforts of life, are not only not indispensable, but positive hindrances to the elevation of mankind."

Thoreau defines two distinct groups of men to whom his advice is addressed: "[first] to the mass of men who are discontented, and idly complaining of the hardness of their lot or of the times, when they might improve them … [and second to] that seemingly wealthy, but most terribly impoverished class of all, who have accumulated dross, but know not how to use it, or get rid of it, and thus have forged their own golden or silver fetters."

Commentary:
The didactic (i.e., intended to instruct) tone established in the first section becomes even more evident. Thoreau examines how quickly in the mind of 'civilized' man a luxury item becomes *regarded as* a necessity. Yet as he becomes more like a lecturer, Thoreau makes greater fun of himself. Having described in detail the "internal combustion" that produces man's "vital heat" and explained death and disease as caused by too rapid burning or by the dying of the fire, he concedes, "Of course the vital heat is not to be confounded with fire; but so much for analogy."

Thoreau's central message is: "The true value of time … is not in producing material goods or services … but in producing spiritual and psychological capital in the form of self-culture" (Schneider in Myerson Ed. 99).

Questions:
5. Examine Thoreau's comic play on words in the phrase "the grossest of groceries"; his self-deprecating humor in the throw-away line "so much for analogy"; the absurdity of the description of men as "luxuriously rich … cooked, of course *à la mode* [i.e., in the fashion]."

"If I should … face of the earth"
Bottom line:
To live in the moment in the contemplation of Nature is the true business or work of life.

Summary:

Thoreau states that the business of his life has always been communion with Nature: "In any weather, at any hour of the day or night, I have been anxious to improve the nick of time, and notch it on my stick too; to stand on the meeting of two eternities, the past and future, which is precisely the present moment; to toe that line."

He states that his business has been weaving ideas and words: "I too had woven a kind of basket of a delicate texture, but I had not made it worth any one's while to buy them. Yet not the less, in my case, did I think it worth my while to weave them, and instead of studying how to make it worth men's while to buy my baskets, I studied rather how to avoid the necessity of selling them." No money was to be made in this business, so he decided to continue with the business for its own sake.

Thoreau gives the rationale behind his experiment in living: "My purpose in going to Walden Pond was not to live cheaply nor to live dearly there, but to transact some private business with the fewest obstacles; to be hindered accomplishing which for want of a little common sense, a little enterprise and business talent, appeared not so sad as foolish."

Commentary:

The opening paragraph arouses expectations of adventure and excitement: "If I should attempt to tell how I have desired to spend my life in years past, it would probably surprise those of my readers who are somewhat acquainted with its actual history; it would certainly astonish those who know nothing about it. I will only hint at some of the enterprises which I have cherished." Thoreau's experiment in living turns out, with comic anti-climax, to have been nothing more than being outside observing Nature and writing about it in a journal that no one else ever read. He has lived what most people would see as a boring and constricted life. It is to correct such a misperception that he writes *Walden*: "The life which men praise and regard as successful is but one kind. Why should we exaggerate any one kind at the expense of the others?"

The use of the words "trade" or "business" to describe how Thoreau used his time is heavily ironic: he appropriates the language of commercialism to describe a self-sufficient life which is its polar opposite since Thoreau's way of living involved minimum consumption and virtually no surplus production. Speaking in 1925, President Coolidge said, "After all, the chief business of the American people is business. They are profoundly concerned with producing, buying, selling, investing and prospering in the world. I am strongly of the opinion that the great majority of people will always find these the moving impulses of our life." It is precisely this view of life that Thoreau sets out to question. *Thoreau* turns the usual meaning of the word 'business' on its head: the purpose of his life has been to experience life to the full, and it was to pursue that purpose with minimum distraction that he went to Walden Pond. The idea that setting up his abode at Walden was a "business" is a comic paradox, for he went there to produce none of those things which a businessman typically produces for sale and financial gain.

Questions:
6. Explain the self-deprecating humor of Thoreau's statement, "For many years I was self-appointed inspector of snow-storms and rain-storms, and did my duty faithfully; surveyor, if not of highways, then of forest paths and all across-lot routes, keeping them open."
7. Since at Walden Pond "you must every where build on piles of your own driving," what exactly does the narrator mean by calling it "a good foundation"? Since Walden Pond is a small, enclosed lake, what exactly does the narrator mean by calling it "a good port"? [The phrase 'a good port' means 'putting in your own foundations'.]
8. What is the point of the vision of the destruction of St. Petersburg that ends this section?

"As this business ... at something high."
Bottom line:
   In his selection and purchasing of clothes, man is more concerned with the opinions of others, with being in the fashion, than with utility.

Summary:
   We need to remember that the only "object of clothing is, first, to retain the vital heat, and secondly, in this state of society, to cover nakedness." Anything else is superfluous.

   We should judge people by their character not their appearance: "No man ever stood the lower in my estimation for having a patch in his clothes; yet I am sure that there is greater anxiety, commonly, to have fashionable, or at least clean and unpatched clothes, than to have a sound conscience."

   In wearing clothes, man "considers, not what is truly respectable, but what is respected ... I say, beware of all enterprises that require new clothes, and not rather a new wearer of clothes. If there is not a new man, how can the new clothes be made to fit? If you have any enterprise before you, try it in your old clothes."

   Instead of dressing in multiple layers, we should recall that "one thick garment is, for most purposes, as good as three thin ones."

   "Every generation laughs at the old fashions, but follows religiously the new." This means that people buy clothes that they *do not need* simply to follow the fashion. This attitude is encouraged by the manufacturers of clothes since it provides a ready market for their wares.

Commentary:
   Thoreau begins by ironically describing his Walden project as a "business

[that] was entered into without the usual capital." In fact, the Walden project was an anti-business having neither capital, raw materials, product or customers. The entire point was to see how life could be lived on the minimum of expenditure and consumption and therefore with the minimum of expenditure.

Having conceded that clothes are one of the few things essential to life, Thoreau next attacks the superfluity of clothes. His mockery of the status quo is full of comic paradoxes: Kings and Queens never wear clothes that fit, clothes that are good enough to worship God in are not regarded as good enough to wear in society, his tailoress cannot make the style of garment he wants because 'They' do not make them anymore, and so on. The section is sprinkled with good jokes: many a man's "life would be ruined" if he should wear trousers patched at the knee, and "clothes introduced sewing, a kind of work you may call endless; a woman's dress, at least, is never done" (a comic play on the old saying 'a woman's work is never done'.)

The section ends on the first real note of social criticism. Thoreau's attack on the system of manufacture which exploits both its customers and its workers "that the corporations may be enriched" might well have found a place in Karl Marx's *Capita* (1867).

Questions:
9. Explain the meaning of Thoreau's comic statement, "The head monkey at Paris puts on a traveller's cap, and all the monkeys in America do the same."
10. The sentence, "When the soldier is hit by a cannonball, rags are as becoming as purple," involves a play on two meanings of the word "purple," the result of which one might call black comedy (humor that appears to trivialize or even mock subject matter usually considered entirely serious, even sacred). What are the two meanings of "purple"? What point is Thoreau making?
11. In the final paragraph of this section, Thoreau expands his attack on the way life is currently lived to a criticism of the means of production: "I cannot believe that our factory system is the best mode by which men may get clothing." [A parallel would be to point out that those technological devices which are so 'essential' to the lives of people today are often the product of the exploitation of poor, underpaid workers in Developing Countries.] What are Thoreau's criticisms of "our factory system"?

"As for a … all the way"
Bottom line:
Modern man invests so great a proportion of his life in securing a shelter and then in furnishing it that he has no time to improve the person who lives *in* that shelter.

Summary:
Shelter is necessary for life, but in civilized societies houses are far bigger

and more elaborate than is strictly necessary, with several consequences. One is that man looses touch with Nature, "we know not what it is to live in the open air…" A second consequence is that, whether a man buys or rents, the cost of maintaining a house is exorbitant, so that, "In the savage state every family owns a shelter as good as the best, and sufficient for its coarser and simpler wants; but … in modern civilized society not more than one half the families own a shelter." As a result, instead of owning, a man rents, which is no better solution in terms of cost, "[I]t is evident that the savage owns his shelter because it costs so little, while the civilized man hires his commonly because he cannot afford to own it; nor can he, in the long run, any better afford to hire."

As proof of this statement, Thoreau reports: "On applying to the assessors, I am surprised to learn that they cannot at once name a dozen in the town who own their farms free and clear." In fact, because of the debts attached to ownership of the property, very few of the farmers in Concord own their farms or ever will do so, "And when the farmer has got his house, he may not be the richer but the poorer for it, and it be the house that has got him."

Money tied up in a house may be seen as a protection against future calamities, but, "I wish to show at what a sacrifice this advantage is at present obtained, and to suggest that we may possibly so live as to secure all the advantage without suffering any of the disadvantage."

True, the majority of people in civilized societies can either own or rent a house, but "civilization has been improving our houses, it has not equally improved the men who are to inhabit them." The minority who can neither afford to own nor rent, actually live in far worse accommodations than did the savages. Even those who live in "moderate circumstances" clutter their houses with fashionable items because "they must have what their neighbors have." They spend all their time keeping their possessions clean and tidy, and so have no time to do the same for their inner selves.

Commentary:
Thoreau suggests a radical definition of "the cost of a thing." We would normally think of this simply in terms of dollars and cents, but Thoreau reminds us that cost is actually "the amount of what I will call life which is required to be exchanged for it, immediately or in the long run."

Thoreau states, "I am far from jesting," but he is being disingenuous (i.e., deliberately deceptive). The argument of this section is consciously exaggerated and the use of comic paradox is extreme: anyone who argues the advantages of having as a shelter a "large box … six feet long by three wide" rather than a house does not expect to be taken *entirely* seriously. Neither can a writer who argues that investing money in a house to pay for one's funeral is irrational since "perhaps a man is not required to bury himself." It is through such obviously absurd arguments that Thoreau wins his reader over to his fundamental point that the pendulum has swung too far in favor of materialism.

Seriousness intrudes when Thoreau is speaking of the shelters provided in modern society for the poor whose labor produces wealth for others. He is particularly bitter in his description of slavery: "I hardly need refer now to the laborers in our Southern States who produce the staple exports of this country, and are themselves a staple production of the South."

Questions:

12. In the paragraph beginning, "It may be guessed…," Thoreau demolishes the argument that the money invested in "superfluous property" is an effective investment against the future. His argument is particularly outrageous. Explain it.
13. How does Thoreau prove the paradox that "our houses are such unwieldy property that we are often imprisoned rather than housed in them"?
14. Explain the comic hyperbole of Thoreau's claim to have been "terrified" to find that the three pieces of limestone on his desk needed to be dusted every day.

"The very simplicity … my own experiment."
Bottom line:

Simplify the material aspects of life in order to maximize the spiritual aspects of life.

Summary:

"The very simplicity and nakedness of man's life in the primitive ages imply this advantage, at least, that they left him still but a sojourner in nature … a taste for the beautiful is most cultivated out of doors, where there is no house and no housekeeper." Men build elaborate houses stuffed with elaborate art, "But lo! men have become the tools of their tools."

In point of fact, it is one of the benefits of man's civilized state that the materials needed to construct, very cheaply, a sufficient dwelling are readily available: "With a little more wit we might use these materials so as to become richer than the richest now are, and make our civilization a blessing."

Commentary:

Although he does not use these terms, Thoreau bemoans the transition of primitive man from hunter gatherer to agriculturalist, for it was this which increased the amount of time that had to be spent in working to raise enough food on which to survive and which, putting an end to the nomadic life, encouraged man to make his shelters more elaborate and so more expensive. Modern society is simply the logical development of a trend begun by that paradigm shift.

Questions:

15. How does Thoreau explain the paradox that, in becoming civilized, "men have become the tools of their tools"?

Walden by Henry David Thoreau

"Near the end … as the Iliad."
Bottom line:
Thoreau found building his cabin to be a cheap, pleasant, and sociable activity.

Summary:
Thoreau describes the building of his house on Walden Pond during March 1845. He stresses that the hours he actually worked were short, the work itself pleasant, and that he was able to observe Nature as he worked.

With borrowed axe, he cut down trees for the frame of his house and constructed the walls with good sound boards purchased for around eight dollars. The work was completed on July 4th – Thoreau leaves the reader to see the significance of the date.

Commentary:
Thoreau makes no claims at all that what he did was either heroic or adventurous. Although he does not mention it, he located his cabin on land owned by his friend Emerson; had he simply trespassed on private property and started cutting down trees, he would have ended up in jail! Also, he makes it clear that he did not build his house from scratch but rather recycled the bulk of his materials from a vacated cabin nearby which he purchased. Finally, he did not achieve all of this building without the help of his neighbors. In these ways, Thoreau shows that his was a *modest experiment* which took place in the real world – a world he shares with the reader.

Work takes place in spring amid signs of rebirth and renewal. When he begins "the ice in the pond was not yet dissolved," but as he works on his cabin the ice on the Pond continually thaws. The building of a cabin represents his own emergence from a spiritual winter: "They were pleasant spring days, in which the winter of man's discontent was thawing itself as well as the earth, and the life that had lain torpid began to stretch itself." He describes a snake which, though it has come out of hibernation, is still not fully awake: it symbolized his own and other men's potential for spiritual awakening. The song of "one early thrush" symbolizes "the higher and more ethereal life" towards which Thoreau is striving.

Questions:
16. Thoreau observes many creatures as he works. Take one example and explain what he learns from the encounter.
17. Thoreau delights in turning conventional values on their head. In this case, conventional wisdom might be represented by Polonius' advice to his son Laertes: "Neither a borrower nor a lender be" (*Hamlet* 1.3). Analyze the deliberate comic inversion of his statement: "It is difficult to begin without borrowing, but perhaps it is the most generous course thus to permit your fellow-men to have an interest in your enterprise."

18. Thoreau does much the same thing when he writes, "At length, in the beginning of May, with the help of some of my acquaintances, rather to improve so good an occasion for neighborliness than from any necessity, I set up the frame of my house." Explain how the joke works here.

"It would be ... in this dirt."

Bottom line:

What we call modern civilized life is on the wrong track entirely, specifically in specializing labor, art and architecture, academic education, and its "'modern improvements.'"

Summary:

This section takes aim at some of the features of civilized life:

- Specialization and the division of labor: "Where is this division of labor to end? and what object does it finally serve? No doubt another may also think for me; but it is not therefore desirable that he should do so to the exclusion of my thinking for myself";
- Architectural ornamentation: "What of architectural beauty I now see, I know has gradually grown from within outward, out of the necessities and character of the indweller, who is the only builder – out of some unconscious truthfulness, and nobleness, without ever a thought for the appearance...";
- The academic education for which the parents of students pay: "I mean that they [young men] should not play life, or study it merely, while the community supports them at this expensive game, but earnestly live it from beginning to end. How could youths better learn to live than by at once trying the experiment of living?";
- Modern improvements in technology (such as the telegraph and the train): "Our inventions are wont to be pretty toys, which distract our attention from serious things."

An inventory of materials and labor is given to determine the cost of Thoreau's cabin. He concludes with mock-serious self-satisfaction, "I intend to build me a house which will surpass any on the main street in Concord in grandeur and luxury, as soon as it pleases me as much and will cost me no more than my present one."

Commentary:

Of course, Thoreau's praise of the simple dwelling of the poor is pure Romanticism which ignores the fact that their dwellings are simple (and often simply wretched) *because* they are poor, and that the lives they lead are more likely to be *truly* desperate than spiritual. The narrator is aware that he is exaggerating to make his point. In this section, he accuses himself of "much cant and hypocrisy," and by doing so preempts any such criticism by the reader.

Anticipating objections that his manner of life was impractical, Thoreau presents his experiment as being successful not only in spiritual but also in economic terms. He describes himself as being a business man who kept a minute record of expenditure and income with which to illustrate that the entire venture was financially profitable. (He is clearly drawing on experience in the family business here.) Thoreau does not intend the reader to take him seriously; the guise of hard-nosed businessman is a comic mask.

Price lists were a common feature of manuals of building and decorating. Thoreau lampoons these lists with his own meticulously calculated list which includes one cent for chalk and is, apparently, correct to the half cent. We are supposed to laugh, not to take it seriously. Any reader who examines the various lists of expenditure will find items missing – not least the fact that he pays no rent on his little farm.

Questions:
19. Why, according to Thoreau, has the word 'carpenter' become "but another name for 'coffinmaker'"?
20. In criticizing the expense of an academic education, Thoreau makes a very good joke, "The consequence is, that while he [the student] is reading Adam Smith, Ricardo, and Say, he runs his father in debt irretrievably." Explain the comedy of this statement (which rests on the academic specialization of Adam Smith, Ricardo, and Jean-Baptiste Say).
21. By what logical argument does Thoreau 'prove' that "the swiftest traveler is he that goes afoot"?

"Before I finished ... may be alarmed."
Bottom line:
Simplify, simplify, simplify – not least in one's diet, for it is the extravagance of diet which leads man to subjugate the animals to labor for him and that leads to some men subjugating other men to labor to produce monuments.

Summary:
Having accounted for the costs of building his cabin, the narrator moves on to living expenses: the result is a section which is part gardening and part cooking guide (all with the narrator's tongue firmly in his cheek).

The key to self-sufficiency is to eat what you grow not to sell what you grow to get money to buy something to eat that someone else grew: "[I]f one would live simply and eat only the crop which he raised, and raise no more than he ate, and not exchange it for an insufficient quantity of more luxurious and expensive things, he would need to cultivate only a few rods of ground, and ... it would be cheaper to spade up that than to use oxen to plow it, and to select a fresh spot from time to time than to manure the old, and he could do all his necessary farm work as it were with his left hand at odd hours in the summer ... I was more independent than any farmer in Concord ..."

Thoreau attacks the system of labor which results in the construction of grand buildings: "It should not be by their architecture, but why not even by their power of abstract thought, that nations should seek to commemorate themselves?"

"I learned from my two years' experience that it would cost incredibly little trouble to obtain one's necessary food, even in this latitude; that a man may use as simple a diet as the animals, and yet retain health and strength."

Commentary:

Certainly Thoreau knows that men are not just going to throw up the benefits of civilization and go to live in the woods on the most bland and basic diet. Of course he does! After all, he himself gave up his experiment after two years, and while in the woods he frequently dined 'out' (i.e., at Emerson's table) as he freely admits. This is all hyperbole to make a point, and his real point is to show the benefits of simplifying one's life *even by a little* and so making room for more time to be spent developing *consciousness of being* – what has more recently been termed 'mindfulness' (i.e., "the practice of maintaining a nonjudgmental state of heightened or complete awareness of one's thoughts, emotions, or experiences on a moment-to-moment basis" [Merriam-Webster]).

Questions:

22. Thoreau loves puns, and here is an example, "I was not anchored to a house or farm, but could follow *the bent* of my genius, which is a very crooked one, every moment" (emphasis added). Explain the play on words.

23. Thoreau loves comic paradox, and the very next sentence furnishes this example, "Beside being better off than they [his neighbors] already, if my house had been burned or my crops had failed, I should have been nearly as well off as before." Explain the apparent paradox that Thoreau was better off than his neighbors despite being manifestly poorer than most.

"My furniture ... they get off."

Bottom line:

A man with more furniture than he needs is like an animal caught in a trap that drags the trap around with him.

Summary:

The narrator described his own modest and inexpensive furniture and bemoans the way in which people keep their surplus furniture which they seem incapable of getting rid of until death, when the burden of ownership is passed on to someone else.

"For more than five years I maintained myself thus solely by the labor of my hands, and I found, that by working about six weeks in a year, I could meet all the expenses of living. The whole of my winters, as well as most of my summers,

I had free and clear for study ... For myself I found that the occupation of a day-laborer was the most independent of any, especially as it required only thirty or forty days in a year to support one. The laborer's day ends with the going down of the sun, and he is then free to devote himself to his chosen pursuit, independent of his labor; but his employer, who speculates from month to month, has no respite from one end of the year to the other."

Commentary:

Having established that he was able to furnish his cabin at minimal expense, Thoreau comments: "None is so poor that he need sit on a pumpkin. That is shiftlessness." This is a delightful piece of mock moralizing. Knowing himself to have been criticized by many in Concord as a mere loafer for living as he did, Thoreau takes the position of a sanctimonious preacher to denounce the shiftless, of whom he is himself (of course) certainly not one.

The comedy is continued by the use of hyperbole: furniture is not a mere inconvenience; it is *evil*, "A lady once offered me a mat, but as I had no room to spare within the house, nor time to spare within or without to shake it, I declined it, preferring to wipe my feet on the sod before my door. It is best to avoid the beginnings of evil." This deliberate overstatement of his case is part of the narrator's defense against the charge that he is taking himself too seriously.

Typical of the way Thoreau turns conventional wisdom on its head is his statement: "It is not necessary that a man should earn his living by the sweat of his brow, unless he sweats easier than I do." Earning a living only becomes a major undertaking requiring time and energy when it comes to mean earning enough money to buy things that you do not need in order to live 'well'.

Questions:

24. The funeral service contains the line, "Ashes to ashes, dust to dust." This provides a fine example of Thoreau's love of comic paradox: "When a man dies he kicks up the dust." What is the argument he uses to maintain the proposition that, far from becoming dust, a dead man stirs up the dust?

25. Referring to the 'primitive' practice of occasionally burning old or superfluous material possessions,
Thoreau comments, "I have no doubt that they were originally inspired directly from Heaven to do thus, though they have no Biblical record of the revelation." Why does he mention Biblical revelation?

"For more than ... they get off."

Bottom line:

Every person must live his own life; it is himself that he has a duty to please, not anyone else.

Summary:

This section reviews how Thoreau discovered the way of earning enough on which to live and to meet his own needs: "For more than five years I maintained myself thus solely by the labor of my hands, and I found that, by working about six weeks in a year, I could meet all the expenses of living. The whole of my winters, as well as most of my summers, I had free and clear for study ... As I preferred some things to others, and especially valued my freedom, as I could fare hard and yet succeed well, I did not wish to spend my time in earning rich carpets or other fine furniture, or delicate cookery, or a house in the Grecian or the Gothic style just yet."

Having experimented with other professions (teaching, trade), Thoreau asserts that for him the best way of earning money was the one which society values least, "I found that the occupation of a day-laborer was the most independent of any, especially as it required only thirty or forty days in a year to support one[self]."

Commentary:

Thoreau is careful to avoid the impression that he is offering a 'one-size-fits-all' solution to how life should be lived. He says: "I desire that there may be as many different persons in the world as possible; but I would have each one be very careful to find out and pursue his own way, and not his father's or his mother's or his neighbor's instead." Not only does the narrator thus evade the accusation that he is trying to dictate to others, Thoreau is laying the foundation for his closing paradox which is that the man who lives the life which truly makes him happy is the man who does most good in the world. Thoreau is a consistent opponent of philanthropy.

Questions:

26. Thoreau takes another shot at the (Protestant American) work ethic, the view that hard work is good in and of itself, "It is not necessary that a man should earn his living by the sweat of his brow, unless he sweats easier than I do." What counter-values does Thoreau place in the balance against the supposed 'nobility of labor'?

"But all this ... like the cypress.'"
Bottom line:

It is better to be good than to do good works – better for the individual and better for society at large.

Summary:

In this section, Thoreau answers a charge commonly made against him that in living a life of isolation on Walden Pond, he did no good to his fellow man – that his was a selfish way of life. Immediately, the narrator turns conventional wisdom on its head by stating that philanthropy is practiced not for the good of those whose suffering is relieved but to make the philanthropist feel better: "But all this [going off into the woods, etc.] is very selfish, I have heard some of my townsmen say. I confess that I have hitherto indulged very little in philanthropic enterprises. I have made some sacrifices to a sense of duty, and among others have sacrificed this pleasure also." Here Thoreau suggests that it is actually philanthropy which is motivated by selfishness.

The argument goes on to make a distinction between *doing* good and *being* good: "What good I do, in the common sense of that word, must be aside from my main path, and for the most part wholly unintended ... Men say ... with kindness aforethought go about doing good ... I should say rather, Set about being good."

Thoreau claims to have discovered the "root" of evil (i.e., the unlived life). Unless we remedy that fault in ourselves, we risk all of our philanthropy producing the kind of misery that we say we strive (in vain) to relieve. Thus, philanthropy "is greatly overrated, and it is our selfishness which overrates it." It originates in man's sense of sorrow and guilt for his failure to feel "a simple and irrepressible satisfaction with the gift of life." He adds: "If I knew for a certainty that a man was coming to my house with the conscious design of doing me good, I should run for my life." [Thoreau today might point out that for all of the billions of dollars spent on charity to relieve poverty around the world that poverty still exists.]

Commentary:

Attack is the best form of defense. The isolated, contemplative life is often criticized as selfish. Thoreau throws this very charge against philanthropy, which is universally admired and respected, arguing that the "do-gooder" is motivated by his "private ail"; that is, that being dissatisfied with his own life, he *diverts* himself by pretending to heal the world. In fact, Thoreau asserts, were all men to cure their "private ail" the world would, incidentally but inevitably, become a much better place. Thoreau's credo is: "let us first be as simple and well as Nature ourselves."

Questions:

27. Exactly why does Thoreau see all philanthropy as at best ineffective and at worst making worse the very ills that it claims to seek to remedy?
28. How do you react to the argument that doing good works for others is ultimately both selfish and counter-productive? Can you give an example?
29. What point is Thoreau making by the reference to the cypress tree?

Chapter Two: Where I lived, and What I lived For

"AT A CERTAIN ... the more at last."
Bottom line:

The vast majority of people have misplaced priorities: they prefer material possessions rather than spiritual purity. Ownership of a house and land is a form of confinement not unlike being in jail.

Summary:

Thoreau describes how, in his imagination, for years he surveyed possible locations for his house, and how, in the case of Hollowell Farm, he came close to actually buying a property attracted by "its complete retirement, being about two miles from the village, half a mile from the nearest neighbour, and separated from the highway." The deal having fallen through, Thoreau was relieved, for though he did not own the land he "retained the landscape," that is, the enjoyment of the land. His considered advice to the reader is to put off settling down and "farming on a large scale" for as long as possible: "I would say to my fellows, once for all, As long as possible live free and uncommitted. It makes but little difference whether you are committed to a farm or the county jail."

Commentary:

This section is a counter-blast to the conventional aspiration to purchase a farm, and thus to own the land on which one builds one's house. The notion that owning a farm is the equivalent of being in jail is deliberately provocative as is the paradoxical statement: "a man is rich in proportion to the number of things which he can afford to let alone."

Questions:

30. What were the qualities that made Hollowell Farm attractive to Thoreau? What do these qualities tell you about the difference between Thoreau's priorities and values and those of his neighbors? Explain what Thoreau means in commenting on his giving up his right to Hollowell Farm: "I found ... that I had been a rich man without any damage to my poverty."

"The present was ... begin to mine."
Bottom line:

Existing is not the same thing as living: "Our life is frittered away by detail ... Simplicity, simplicity, simplicity! I say, let your affairs be as two or three, and not a hundred or a thousand ... Simplify, simplify ... Why should we live with such hurry and waste of life? ... "

Summary:

Thoreau describes the location of his cabin on Walden Pond and how he lived there sensitive to the rhythms of the day, not at the mercy of the factory bell. He sought to live a life where: "Every morning was a cheerful invitation to make my life of equal simplicity, and I may say innocence, with Nature herself." Bathing in the Pond was like baptism – a physically and spiritually invigorating birth into life itself. *He believed in living a simple life*

The following sentences are probably the most famous in the entire book. Here is Thoreau's credo: "I went to the woods because I wished to live deliberately, to front only the essential facts of life, and see if I could not learn what it had to teach, and not, when I came to die, discover that I had not lived. I did not wish to live what was not life, living is so dear; nor did I wish to practise resignation, unless it was quite necessary. I wanted to live deep and suck out all the marrow of life, to live so sturdily and Spartan-like as to put to rout all that was not life, to cut a broad swath and shave close, to drive life into a corner, and reduce it to its lowest terms, and, if it proved to be mean, why then to get the whole and genuine meanness of it, and publish its meanness to the world; or if it were sublime, to know it by experience, and be able to give a true account of it in my next excursion."

Thoreau goes on to question the purposes for which men build railroads, communicate by telegraph, write letters, and read newspapers. [Today, he would include television, radio, the Internet, social media, computer games, cell phones, and much more.] In terms of 'cost-benefit analysis,' Thoreau concludes that little is gained at the incalculable cost of expending our lives: "I perceive that we inhabitants of New England live this mean life that we do because our vision does not penetrate the surface of things. We think that that *is* which *appears* to be."

Just as each man should strive to maintain the state of consciousness that he experiences in the first hour of every morning, before the tasks of the day have dulled his sense of what life might be, so he should strive to be as he was when he was born: "I have always been regretting that I was not as wise as the day I was born. The intellect is a cleaver; it discerns and rifts its way into the secret of things. I do not wish to be any more busy with my hands than is necessary." Thoreau criticizes the frantic pace of modern life focusing particularly on the impact of the news media (telegraph, letters, newspapers). As a result, he argues "we inhabitants of New England live this mean life that we do because our vision does not penetrate the surface of things. We think that that *is* which *appears* to be." In contrast, Thoreau wants to live each day *in* the day without distractions: "Let us spend one day as deliberately as Nature, and not be thrown off the track by every nutshell and mosquito's wing that falls on the rails. Let us rise early and fast, or break fast, gently and without perturbation; let company come and let company go, let the bells ring and the children cry, – determined to make a day of it."

Commentary:

Thoreau's aim in writing *Walden* is expressed in the famous image that opens this section, "I do not propose to write an ode to dejection, but to brag as lustily as chanticleer [i.e., a rooster] in the morning, standing on his roost, if only to wake my neighbors up." [This sentence also appeared on the title page of the first edition of *Walden* just under a drawing of Thoreau's cabin.] The simile suggests that Thoreau is proud of what he has to communicate, knows its value, and is confident that he can lead his readers to live a fuller life. On the other hand, there is an element of comic hyperbole in the simile: everyone knows (or can imagine) how irritating being woken at the crack of dawn by a rooster can be (the alarm clock is but a pale imitation). Knowing that the pedagogic tone of his book must appear to many to be arrogant, Thoreau forestalls criticism by announcing loudly with pride that he has something of importance to say.

"I got up early and bathed in the pond; that was a religious exercise, and one of the best things which I did," Thoreau writes. In calling his morning wash in the pond "a religious exercise," he is reflecting the Transcendentalist origins of his philosophy in a way which he knows will shock his Protestant neighbors. His morning bathe in the Pond is a form of baptism in Nature, a spiritual purification.

To illustrate how ethereal are the tasks with which man fills daily life, he postulates a fire in the village which would call every man instantly from his 'work,' thus proving how worthless that work really was. He adds of his hypothetical house-fire "we, be it known, did not set it on fire." This is a self-deprecating reference to the time when, in April 1843, Thoreau *did* set on fire a good portion of the Walden woods, an act of carelessness for which many in the locality never forgave him. (He refers to this embarrassing incident at least once more in the book. Look out for the reference.)

As always, Thoreau calls in question the 'received wisdom' about how life should be lived: "Men say that a stitch in time saves nine, and so they take a thousand stitches to-day to save nine to-morrow." Here he returns to his theme that men live their lives in preparation for some future catastrophe and so do not live their lives at all.

Thoreau ends with a description of himself as a miner searching for "the richest vein." This is the last of several metaphors in this chapter all describing the inward journey into one's own consciousness that was facilitated by spare time and being surrounded by Nature. In Thoreau's view, the individual consciousness becomes the center around which the world arranges itself. He refuses to simply 'fit in' to a predetermined pattern (whether it be cultural, social, legal, economic or religious). Verse three of the Anglican hymn *All Things Bright and Beautiful* (1848) embodies the rationale for the pervading social determinism that Thoreau is rejecting:

> The rich man in his castle,
> The poor man at his gate,
> God made them high and lowly,
> And ordered their estate

Questions:

31. "To be awake is to be alive. I have never yet met a man who was quite awake. How could I have looked him in the face?" Explain what Thoreau means by that question.

32. How should a man go about retaining 'birth-consciousness' or 'morning consciousness' throughout his life?

33. Of what inventions, modern in Thoreau's time, does he question the value? (Of what contemporary inventions would *you* question the value?)

34. Thoreau's love of paradox is illustrated in the following description of railroads and how they are constructed: "We do not ride on the railroad; it rides upon us. Did you ever think what those sleepers are that underlie the railroad? Each one is a man, an Irishman, or a Yankee man. The rails are laid on them, and they are covered with sand, and the cars run smoothly over them. They are sound sleepers, I assure you." ('Sleepers' are, of course, the sturdy timbers on which the railway lines are laid.) What does Thoreau mean by saying that the 'railroad … rides upon us," and that the "sleepers" are the dead bodies of the navvies who built the railroads? Explain the play on words in the phrase "sound sleepers."

35. Thoreau writes, "We think that that *is* which *appears* to be" (original emphasis). Explain what he means.

36. "Time is but the stream I go a-fishing in." Explain how this sentence sums up the attitude to living that Thoreau is seeking to achieve.

37. What does Thoreau mean when he writes: "My head is hands and feet"?

Chapter Three: Reading

Bottom line:
Reading the classics, preferably in the original Greek or Latin, is to access "the treasured wealth and the fit inheritance of generations and nations ... In dealing with truth we are immortal."

Summary:
The cabin in the woods provides the perfect environment for reflective, contemplative reading. The pursuit of knowledge and understanding of the self is to invest one's life in truths which defy the passage of time: "In accumulating property for ourselves or our posterity, in founding a family or a state, or acquiring fame even, we are mortal; but in dealing with truth we are immortal, and need fear no change nor accident."

Although up to this point Thoreau has rejected the conventional 'wisdom' of previous generations as antithetical to the spiritual growth of the individual, he now makes a significant exception stating that: "books are the treasured wealth of the world and the fit inheritance of generations and nations." It is in the classics of literature that man encounters "the noblest recorded thoughts of man," but such books must be read "as deliberately and reservedly as they were written." Then, and then only is reading "a noble exercise." He describes the classics as being "as beautiful almost as the morning itself," recalling his description of his daily baptism in the waters of the Pond.

This is not the kind of reading for which most men have been prepared by their education: "Most men
have learned to read to serve a paltry convenience, as they have learned to cipher in order to keep
accounts and not be cheated in trade; but of reading as a noble intellectual exercise they know little or nothing; yet this only is reading, in a high sense, not that which lulls us as a luxury and suffers the nobler faculties to sleep the while, but what we have to stand on tip-toe to read and devote our most alert and wakeful hours to."

As a result, even those in Concord who regard themselves as being educated do not read the classics of prose and poetry: "We are underbred and low-lived and illiterate; and in this respect I confess I do not make any very broad distinction between the illiterateness of my townsman who cannot read at all and the illiterateness of him who has learned to read only what is for children and feeble intellects."

Thoreau paints a picture of what Concord *could be* – a community dedicated to life-long learning: "It is time that villages were universities, and their elder inhabitants the fellows of universities, with leisure – if they are, indeed, so well off – to pursue liberal studies the rest of their lives."

Walden by Henry David Thoreau

Commentary:

Readers will perhaps fairly accuse Thoreau of intellectual elitism (we can't all have gone to Harvard!) as he bemoans the current state of literature, education and reading, and insists that the classics *must* be read in their original language. In doing so, he gives an almost mystical importance to the printed word. Certainly, his contemporaries might have been offended by his criticism of those whose reading of ancient writers never goes beyond the Bible: "Most men do not know that any nation but the Hebrews have had a scripture." Here we see that Thoreau's conception of religion includes, but entirely transcends, Christianity – an idea that he knows to be offensive to most of his readers. He also attacks the newspapers and the 'cheap' fiction and non-fiction of the day commenting: "The best books are not read even by those who are called good readers." His neighbors might reasonably have pointed out that Thoreau's ability to read Latin and Greek was the result of his privileged birth – a thought which seems not to occur to the narrator.

However, against those who see Thoreau as an elitist is his plea that Concord should spend more money on education for the benefit of *all* of its citizens. Notice how the chapter begins as personal reportage (first person singular – "I") and ends by speaking for the community (first person plural – "We"). Thus, some of the offensive edge is taken off his criticism when he includes himself amongst those he criticizes: "*We* are under-bred and low-lived and illiterate; and in this respect I confess I do not make any very broad distinction between the illiterateness of my townsman who cannot read at all, and the illiterateness of him who has learned to read only what is for children and feeble intellects" (emphasis added). His vision of Concord as a 'learning community' is idealistic nonsense, but one suspects that he knows that: the aim is to move Concord (and all of the Concords throughout the world) just *a step or two* in the right direction. The social reform advocated here makes it quite clear that Thoreau is not advocating that each of his readers should replicate his experiment of living isolated in the woods; rather, he wants them to apply the insights he gained there to their lives as members of society.

Questions:

38. Analyze the bride image in the final sentence of this chapter.

Chapter Four: Sounds

Bottom line:

Time spent simply looking and listening to the sounds of the world (both natural and man-made) is time well spent. By "looking always at what is to be seen," boredom becomes impossible.

Summary:

Throwing aside consistency, Thoreau now downplays book reading saying: "I did not read books the first summer; I hoed beans." He seems to feel that he had already done the requisite reading before he came to Walden Pond. Literature is no substitute for reality because writing is just a dialect of "the language which all things and events speak without metaphor, [and] which alone is copious and standard." This he seeks to experience by always being alert to his surroundings and by practicing "the discipline of looking always at what is to be seen [and heard]"

"What is a course of history or philosophy, or poetry, no matter how well selected, or the best society,
or the most admirable routine of life, compared with the discipline of looking always at what is to be seen? Will you be a reader, a student merely, or a seer? Read your fate, see what is before you, and walk on into futurity."

He then describes the sounds of a typical day: the morning birds; the afternoon train and on Sundays the church bells of neighboring towns; in the evening the cows, the whippoorwills, and owls. Regularly: "The whistle of the locomotive penetrates my woods summer and winter, sounding like the scream of a hawk sailing over some farmer's yard, informing me that many restless city merchants are arriving within the circle of the town, or adventurous country traders from the other side." This prompts reflection on the impact of the railway on society. As much as Thoreau tries to accept this sound in the way that he does the sounds of Nature (note the simile of the hawk above and compare the simile of the rattling cars sounding "like the beat of a partridge"), he ultimately fails. He attempts to feel that the sound of the train is as baptismal as bathing and reading: "I am refreshed and expanded when the freight train rattles past me, and I smell the stores which go dispensing their odors all the way from Long Wharf to Lake Champlain, reminding me of foreign parts, of coral reefs, and Indian oceans, and tropical climes, and the extent of the globe. I feel more like a citizen of the world ..." However, we should not take this seriously: Thoreau is *parodying* the extravagant praise that his contemporaries constantly heaped on technological progress and the consequent improvement of society. He finally admits that he cannot reconcile this product of the Industrial Revolution with the world of Nature that he inhabits: it is something alien and destructive. He concludes: "I will not have my eyes put out and my ears spoiled by its smoke, and steam, and hissing."

Walden by Henry David Thoreau

The train past, Thoreau was free to listen to the bells of distant towns, the lowing of a cow in a pasture beyond the woods, the songs of whippoorwills, and in the evening the hooting of the owls. His sense of wholeness returns, though still there is in the distance the faint sound of railway wagons.

Next he lists the sounds he did *not* hear: no rooster woke him; no domesticated animals disturbed him; no sounds of domestic industry. In fact, nothing except "unfenced nature reaching up to your very sills."

Commentary:

The first few paragraphs are full of metaphors that link Thoreau's spiritual purification with the sensual experience of Nature. Thus, he writes: "There were times when I could not afford to sacrifice the bloom of the present moment to any work, whether of the head or hands." Spiritually, he says that he: "grew in those seasons like corn in the night." As Nature comes back to life in the spring so does Thoreau: "The large buds, suddenly pushing out late in the spring from dry sticks which had seemed to be dead, developed themselves as by magic into graceful green and tender boughs."

Any idea that Thoreau was some sort of wild man seeking to cut himself off from 'civilization' is dispelled in this chapter. He is honest enough to admit that there is no place in Massachusetts that remains isolated from the 'modern' world: the time when one could actually get away from the influence of trade and technology is long past.

The unnatural, mechanical sound of the railway intrudes upon his communion with Nature. Having failed to integrate this industrial sound with the sounds emanating from the natural world, he turns to satire: "When I hear the iron horse make the hills echo with his snort-like thunder, shaking the earth with his feet, and breathing fire and smoke from his nostrils . . . it *seems* as if the earth had got a race now worthy to inhabit it. If all were as it *seems*, and men made the elements their servants for noble ends" (emphasis added). What Thoreau is doing here is parodying the prevailing view of the 'brave new world' of technology and commerce (just as elsewhere he parodies the balance sheet approach of the self-help books of the period). The problem is that, whereas with Nature appearance and reality are the same, with industry and commerce it is *not* so. Though he continues to say a great deal that is positive about the railway, the intention is ironic: "What recommends commerce to me is its enterprise and bravery ... I see these men every day go about their business with more or less courage and content, doing more even than they suspect, and perchance better employed than they could have consciously devised ... I feel more like a citizen of the world at the sight of the palm-leaf which will cover so many flaxen New England heads the next summer..." This is comic hyperbole about which we may judge, with Queen Gertrude, that he "doth protest too much" (*Hamlet*). For Thoreau, the problem is that all of this apparently 'heroic' spirit is used for the ignoble end of moving materials around the country (even around the globe) and in the process trivializing the lives of those who sell and buy them and come to depend upon them. (In the same way, he earlier pointed to education only enabling people to read trashy books.) The locomotive is simply a facilitator of that consumer culture that Thoreau blames for robbing life of its spiritual quality, and so it represents everything that he came to the woods to fight in his own life. The industrialization of America has destroyed the Jeffersonian ideal of the agrarian way of life that the narrator prefers because it had the potential to keep man in contact with Nature.

Questions:

39. How does Thoreau defend himself against the accusation of many of his "fellow-townsmen" that his way of life on Walden Pond was "sheer idleness"?

40. In the course of his ironic defense of the railroad, Thoreau makes probably the best joke in the whole book: "Commerce is unexpectedly confident and serene, alert, adventurous, and unwearied. It is very natural in its methods withal, far more so than *many fantastic enterprises and sentimental experiments*, and hence its singular success." Explain how Thoreau is making fun of himself here. (Clue: Look at the words I have emphasised.)

41. As a carload of sheep rattle by, Thoreau describes "a car-load of drovers, too, in the midst, on a level with their droves now, their vocation gone, but still clinging to their useless sticks as their badge of office." Explain the significance of this observation.

42. In the final pages of this chapter ("And hark! ... civilized world!"), Thoreau describes hearing various sounds some generated by humans and others by animals. To which sounds does he attach a symbolic value?

Chapter Five: Solitude

Bottom line:

You are never lonesome when you are alone in and with Nature: "I come and go with a strange liberty in Nature, a part of herself … Am I not partly leaves and vegetable mould myself?"

Summary:

Thoreau opens with a description of how it feels to have achieved mystical union with Nature: "This is a delicious evening, when the whole body is one sense, and imbibes delight through every pore. I go and come with a strange liberty in Nature, a part of herself."

The situation of Thoreau's cabin seems to him ideal, for although he can see no other habitation from it he is less than a mile from his neighbors who visit him and, if he is absent, leave some token of their call.

His true society is, however, the natural world that surrounds him and the opportunity which the isolated position of his cabin gives him to commune with Nature: "I have never felt lonesome, or in the least oppressed by a sense of solitude, but once, and that was a few weeks after I came to the woods, when, for an hour, I doubted if the near neighborhood of man was not essential to a serene and healthy life. To be alone was something unpleasant. But I was at the same time conscious of a slight insanity in my mood, and seemed to foresee my recovery. In the midst of a gentle rain while these thoughts prevailed, I was suddenly sensible of such sweet and beneficent society in Nature, in the very pattering of the drops, and in every sound and sight around my house, an infinite and unaccountable friendliness all at once like an atmosphere sustaining me, as made the fancied advantages of human neighborhood insignificant, and I have never thought of them since."

The secret of Thoreau's contentment is that he is happy *doing nothing* – just sitting in his doorway watching the rain for hour after hour. To Thoreau, this is *not* wasted time: this is what makes him so different from his neighbors who must always either be doing something 'productive' or with someone to take their minds off being alone.

The farmer at work never feels lonely, but in the evening he feels that he needs human company. In contrast, Thoreau values the time when rain stops him from working on his beans and allows him the opportunity for contemplation: "I find it wholesome to be alone the greater part of the time. To be in company, even with the best, is soon wearisome and dissipating. I love to be alone. I never found the companion that was so companionable as solitude. We are for the most part more lonely when we go abroad among men than when we stay in our chambers. A man thinking or working is always alone, let him be where he will. Solitude is not measured by the miles of space that intervene between a man and his fellows."

Finally, Thoreau praises the healthful benefits of Nature (which he represents as female, the goddess Hebe, bringer of the spring) and of his deep communion with it: "I go and come with a strange liberty in Nature, a part of herself." This, rather than man's medicines, is the true source of vigor and health. He asks the rhetorical question: "What is the pill which will keep us well, serene, contented?"

Commentary:

The title of the chapter is ironic. Thoreau does not write about *his* "solitude" at all because living on the Pond he lives in divine companionship with Nature which is the living embodiment of the Creator. He has shunned human company for what he calls a "more normal and natural society." To be in harmony with Nature makes Thoreau spiritually whole something that he has found human company to be incapable of doing.

Thoreau begins by enumerating in detail the animals in whose company he spends his days and concludes positively: "There can be no very black melancholy to him who lives in the midst of Nature and has his senses still." Then he points out that in reality (his house being only one mile from his closest neighbor) there were plenty of callers. Since he was usually away from his cabin when they called, they left some token of their visit: "When I return to my house I find that visitors have been there and left their cards, either a bunch of flowers, or a wreath of evergreen, or a name in pencil on a yellow walnut leaf or a chip." The reference to visiting cards is an ironic swipe at the complex etiquette of visiting which pervaded the polite society of his day.

A superficial reading of this chapter supports the stereotype of Thoreau as an anti-social recluse. Nothing could be further from the truth. It is, Thoreau argues, *society* which undervalues companionship, making it so common by forcing people to live almost constantly in close proximity to others, so that they have nothing of value to say to each other. As a result their interactions are trivial and meaningless. Solitude is not at all the same as loneliness; it is the prerequisite for communion with Nature, of becoming a part of that of which we *are* a part: "While I enjoy the friendship of the seasons I trust that nothing can make life a burden to me."

Questions:

43. Explain the paradox, "I have a great deal of company in my house; especially in the morning, when nobody calls."
44. A local farmer asks Thoreau "how I could bring myself to give up so many of the comforts of life." How does Thoreau make it clear that it is the farmer, not himself, who has done this?
45. Thoreau describes in detail receiving evening visits from an "old settler" and an "elderly dame." What is your sense of the nature of these visitors?

Chapter Six: Visitors

"I THINK THAT ... the other side."
Bottom line:

Seeing people often and being physically close to them actually limits genuine communication.

Summary:

Thoreau immediately attacks precisely the stereotype of him that so many people have: "I THINK THAT I love society as much as most, and am ready enough to fasten myself like a bloodsucker for the time to any full-blooded man that comes in my way. I am naturally no hermit ..." The question is, however, what would actually constitute a "full-blooded man," for our narrator clearly does not suffer fools gladly.

The chapter is full of paradoxes. Physical proximity is not the same thing as genuine communication. The two are entirely unconnected: "I have had twenty-five or thirty souls, with their bodies, at once under my roof, and yet we often parted without being aware that we had come very near to one another." In other words, the people so crowded together had nothing of any consequence to say to each other. Physical proximity does not allow the space between people which is required "to utter big thoughts in big words"; it promotes trivialities. Thus, it is society which is truly unsociable; the narrator claims to have a truly sociable character.

Words, Thoreau deems, a poor substitute for real communication: "If we would enjoy the most intimate society with that in each of us which is without, or above, being spoken to, we must not only be silent, but commonly so far apart bodily that we cannot possibly hear each other's voice in any case. Referred to this standard, speech is for the convenience of those who are hard of hearing; but there are many fine things which we cannot say if we have to shout."

Nevertheless, since "men ... will hardly fail on anywhere," Thoreau did have visitors though he made no effort to offer them dinner as is the expectation in society, for he had little enough for himself. In all, he had more *real* visitors than at any time in his life because men had to make a particular effort to come out to his cabin so that "fewer came upon trivial business."

Commentary:

Thoreau has earlier satirized the social fashion of leaving one's calling card – his visitors generally left more natural records of their having been in his cabin while he was away. Now, he turns to the etiquette which dictates that a visitor must be fed, and that a host will be judged on the quality of his dinners. With one guest, he might share his food, but with many neither he nor they ate, which he turns into a typical joke, "if any ever went away disappointed or hungry from my house when they found me at home, they may depend upon it that I sympathized with them at least." He means that, by the end of the visit, he was as hungry as were his visitors!

Questions:

46. How does Thoreau justify the assertion: "I had more visitors while I lived in the woods than at any other period in my life..."?

"Who should come ... dark and muddy."

Bottom line:

Satisfaction with self and with one's lifestyle is the enemy of intellectual and spiritual growth.

Summary:

The Canadian wood-chopper is a regular visitor, a man skilled at his work but with no interest in introspection, serious reading or self-improvement: "A more simple and natural man it would be hard to find ... In him the animal man chiefly was developed. In physical endurance and contentment he was cousin to the pine and the rock ... But the intellectual and what is called spiritual man in him were slumbering as in an infant." In this, Thoreau finds the Canadian typical of most men.

The wood-chopper is an example of a man who has dedicated his entire being to physical labor which fills his time to the exclusion of self-reflection and communion with Nature. In this way, Thoreau considers work to be a negative in his existence: "He would say, as he went by in the morning, 'How thick the pigeons are! If working every day were not my trade, I could get all the meat I should want by hunting-pigeons, woodchucks, rabbits, partridges – by gosh! I could get all I should want for a week in one day ... a man that has to work as I do, if he does not forget the ideas he has had, he will do well. May be the man you hoe with is inclined to race; then, by gorry, your mind must be there; you think of weeds.'"

Nevertheless, Thoreau detects a "certain positive originality" in the man's thought, though he laments that "I never, by any manoeuvring could get him to take the spiritual view of things." Thoreau concludes of his acquaintance with the wood-chopper: "He suggested that there might be men of genius in the lowest grades of life, however permanently humble and illiterate ..." The man has unfulfilled potential.

[The wood-chopper was actually a man called Alex Therien. The Spark Notes editors say of him, "Unlike Thoreau, Therien cannot read or write" – one of their few errors since the text explicitly says that he can do both. However, he decodes the words without penetrating their meaning, and he writes words without using writing as a stimulus to self-reflection.]

Commentary:

This is one of those sections which critics love to use against Thoreau accusing him of being a snob in his condescending description of the Canadian. There is certainly something in this, but you will find plenty of times that the narrator pays tribute to the man's natural intelligence. What pains Thoreau is not that the man exists on the level of an animal, but that in doing so he is wasting his full, human potential. Thoreau largely blames the priests who educated the man because they made him passive and accepting never seeking to educate him "to the degree of consciousness, but only to the degree of trust and reverence…"

Questions:
47. How does the final paragraph of this section change your view of the Canadian?

"Many a traveller … with that race."
Bottom line:
   You meet a better class of visitor when you live alone in the woods.

Summary:
   Thoreau records, somewhat ruefully, that people frequently came to see him out of idle curiosity. Many who came were those defined by society as 'intellectually challenged.' Typically, the narrator turns this judgment on its head: "Half-witted men from the almshouse and elsewhere came to see me; but I endeavored to make them exercise all the wit they had … Indeed, I found some of them to be wiser than the so-called overseers of the poor and selectmen of the town, and thought it was time that the tables were turned." The only visitors he would not tolerate were beggars, those who "are resolved, for one thing never to help themselves." He concludes definitively: "Objects of charity are not guests."
   Following his theme of the negative impact of 'business' upon the human capacity to live, Thoreau makes an important distinction based on his observation. Women and children appear to be more at home in the woods than businessmen or farmers: "Girls and boys and young women generally seemed glad to be in the woods. They looked in the pond and at the flowers, and improved their time. Men of business, even farmers, thought only of solitude and employment … Restless committed men, whose time was all taken up in getting a living or keeping it …"
   Thoreau notes that the old and the infirm are so concentrated on their mortality, and on staying alive for as long as possible, that they live in constant fear and therefore do not live at all. He concludes: "if a man is alive, there is always danger that he may die, though the danger must be allowed to be less in proportion as he is dead-and-alive to begin with."

Commentary:
   Paradox upon comic paradox: the civic leaders have less wit than the half-witted, the men committed to making a good living have no life at all, and those

who constantly fear death have do not allow themselves to live. No wonder Thoreau offended some of his contemporaries!

Questions:

48. What does Thoreau mean when he says that he encountered "one real runaway slave"? (Clue: Focus on the word "real.")

49. Thoreau says jokingly that he feared not "the hen-harriers" but did fear "the men-harriers." Explain what he means.

Chapter Seven: The Bean-Field

Bottom line:
Planting and hoeing beans is not a means to an end but an end in itself.

Summary:
In planting and hoeing his beans, Thoreau attracted the attention of passing travelers, the company of woodland creatures, and felt close to those who had formerly inhabited the area: "As I drew a still fresher soil about the rows with my hoe, I disturbed the ashes of unchronicled nations who in primeval years lived under these heavens, and their small implements of war and hunting were brought to the light of this modern day." Unlike farmers who work only for a financial gain, Thoreau enjoyed and felt spiritually fulfilled by his work.

From the town, he heard evidence of military training and display (he refers to the Mexican American War which he opposed): "When there was a military turnout of which I was ignorant, I have sometimes had a vague sense all the day of some sort of itching and disease in the horizon, as if some eruption would break out there soon..."

After having worked on his beans very hard during his first summer, Thoreau speaks of wanting to spend less time doing so during his second summer, and records his sense of having failed to use the resulting freed time productively: "I said to myself, I will not plant beans and corn with so much industry another summer, but such seeds, if the seed is not lost, as sincerity, truth, simplicity, faith, innocence, and the like, and see if they will not grow in this soil, even with less toil and manurance, and sustain me, for surely it has not been exhausted for these crops. Alas! I said this to myself; but now another summer is gone, and another, and another, and I am obliged to say to you, Reader, that the seeds which I planted, if indeed they were the seeds of those virtues, were wormeaten or had lost their vitality, and so did not come up." This is an age which attends to work rather than to working on the mind.

Commentary:
The bean-field begins as a symbol of the narrator's inner self, and his near-obsession with cutting out the weeds represents his effort to simplify and purify his life and so his being. It is also useful to read this account of planting and hoeing beans as an extended metaphor for writing, which was the means by which Thoreau 'found himself' – it was, after all, the need to write that brought Thoreau to Walden. Imagine the rows of beans as lines of writing and the hoeing as the writer revising them, and it all makes sense. Symbolic of the freedom that he achieved in his activity are the birds that he records having seen as he hoed: "[T]he night-hawk circled overhead ... small imps that fill the air ... a pair of hen-hawks circling high ... the passage of wild pigeons ... [all] part of the inexhaustible entertainment which the country offers."

However, "Beans" soon become a symbol for worldly possessions. Perhaps Thoreau has in mind the idiomatic phrase, '[It didn't] amount to a hill of beans' meaning nothing of any significance. He writes that, "Most men I do not meet at all, for they seem not to have time; they are busy about their beans." Ironically, even the farmers, who one might expect to be close to Nature are too concerned with productivity actually to experience Nature: "By avarice and selfishness, and a grovelling habit, from which none of us is free, of regarding the soil as property, or the means of acquiring property chiefly, the landscape is deformed, husbandry is degraded with us, and the farmer leads the meanest of lives. He knows Nature but as a robber." Perhaps Thoreau found himself in danger of making the same error, and this accounts for his determination during his second summer to spend less of his time cultivating beans.

The reader will notice that the balance sheets are correct to the half cent, and may recall that those in Chapter One are correct to the quarter cent. Even the contemporary reader must suspect he/she is having his leg pulled here – accounting for inflation, a cent was not worth very much in Thoreau's day. What is less obvious is that the narrator is satirizing the 'How to...' manuals of his day (as in '... build a house,' '... plant a garden,' etc.) which always listed expenditure precisely (though not quite *this* precisely).

Questions:
50. Thoreau writes rather mystically of his experience, "It was no longer beans that I hoed, nor I that hoed beans." Explain what he means.

Chapter Seven: The Village
Bottom line:
The village was a place to visit; the best part was returning to the woods and losing oneself in the darkness of the night.

Summary:
Even after manual work or intellectual study, Thoreau needed to bathe once again in the purifying waters of the Pond.

Thoreau records his regular visits to Concord and that, in small doses, its gossip proved stimulating.
He describes the village as an anthropologist would, as an impartial and objective observer – in fact, with the same detachment with which he describes Nature. He notes groups of bored men with nothing to do avid for the latest piece of gossip.

The main attraction of the village was, however, leaving it at night in the darkness to make his way back to his cabin: "It is a surprising and memorable, as well as valuable experience, to be lost in the woods any time ... not till we are completely lost, or turned round ... do we appreciate the vastness and strangeness of Nature ... Not till we are lost, in other words not till we have lost the world, do we begin to find ourselves, and realize where we are and the infinite extent of our relations." To see the world anew means freeing oneself of all of the preconceptions about what society should be and what the individual ought to value.

Thoreau records in passing his arrest, on one of his visits to Concord, for failure to pay a poll tax to a state which held slavery to be legal, a "state that buys and sells men, women, and children, like cattle at the door of its senate-house."

He concludes, somewhat idealistically; "I am convinced, that if all men were to live as simply as I then did, thieving and robbery would be unknown. These take place only in communities where some have got more than is sufficient while others have not enough."

Commentary:

Thoreau loses a few more friends by making fun of the 'gossip mill' that is Concord and of those who have apparently nothing better to do than to participate in it.

In this chapter, particularly towards the end, Thoreau comes closest to the political polemic [i.e., attack] of his essay *Resistance to Civil Government* (1849) [reprinted as *Civil Disobedience* in 1866] where he wrote: "I heartily accept the motto, – 'That government is best which governs least;' and I should like to see it acted up to more rapidly and systematically. Carried out, it finally amounts to this, which I also believe, – 'That government is best which governs not at all;' and when men are prepared for it, that will be the kind of government which they will have. Government is at best but an expedient; but most governments are usually, and all governments are sometimes, inexpedient." His is what we should not call a Libertarian view. Government should not force anyone to do or believe anything; it should guide men by good example alone: "You who govern public affairs, what need have you to employ punishments? Love virtue, and the people will be virtuous." Much as one sympathizes with Thoreau's opposition to government sponsored slavery and wars of aggression, his vision of an ideal society is just that – unrealistic.

Questions:

51. What were the "dangers" from which Thoreau reports himself as having "escaped wonderfully"?

52. Thoreau writes, "Not till we are lost, in other words, not till we have lost the world, do we begin to find ourselves." Explain why he could not 'find himself' in Concord.

Chapter Eight: The Ponds

SOMETIMES, HAVING HAD … the ocean wave?"
Bottom line:
The unique beauties of Walden Pond are described.

Summary:

This is the most descriptive chapter yet and the least discursive. In it the reader sees Thoreau the naturalist painting a picture of the immediate environment of his cabin. Thoreau describes fishing at midnight on Walden Pond and hooking both fish and ideas: "It was very queer, especially in dark nights, when your thoughts had wandered to vast and cosmogonal [i.e., relating to the cosmos or universe] themes in other spheres, to feel this faint jerk, which came to interrupt your dreams and link you to Nature again. It seemed as if I might next cast my line upward into the air, as well as downward into this element, which was scarcely more dense. Thus I caught two fishes as it were with one hook."

He describes the color of the Pond, the purity of its water, the fluctuating water levels over long periods of time, the (unexplained) path clear of vegetation that goes around it, the coldness of the water, and the fish and animals that inhabit its borders.

Thoreau again sets himself at odds with his neighbors firstly by preferring time he spent on the Pond to the time he should have spent earning: "Many a forenoon have I stolen away, preferring to spend thus the most valued part of the day; for I was rich, if not in money, in sunny hours and summer days, and spent them lavishly; nor do I regret that I did not waste more of them in the workshop or the teacher's desk"; and secondly by chiding his neighbors both for chopping down so many of the trees that sixty years before made the Pond "dark with surrounding forest," and for having the idea of piping the water of the Pond to Concord: "Now the trunks of trees on the bottom, and the old log canoe, and the dark surrounding woods, are gone, and the villagers, who scarcely know where it lies, instead of going to the pond to bathe or drink, are thinking to bring its water, which should be as sacred as the Ganges at least, to the village in a pipe, to wash their dishes with! – to earn their Walden by the turning of a cock or drawing of a plug!" Despite these incursions, Walden "wears best, and best preserves its purity … [and] is perennially young."

Commentary:

Thoreau opens with two examples of the failure of conventional life. Commercially picked, transported and marketed berries, such as the residents of Boston buy, he assures us, lose their "ambrosial and essential part." Next he describes those who fished unsuccessfully all day on the Pond whom Thoreau groups with "the ancient sect of Cœnobites." The historian of ancient theology will recognize a reference to religious communities, but the alert reader will recognize a pun of 'See-no-bites' implying that they wasted their time! In contrast, Thoreau reports himself as hooking both physical fish and abstract ideas as he drifted on the Pond at night.

The description of Walden Pond stresses the purity its water: "[The pond is] remarkable for its depth and purity ... it is a clear and deep green well ... this water is of such crystalline purity ... so transparent that the bottom can easily be discerned at a depth of twenty-five or thirty feet ... the bottom is pure sand ... it is pure at all times ... all the fishes which inhabit this pond are much cleaner, handsomer, and firmer fleshed than those in the river and most other ponds, as the water is purer." The Pond appears to be a living entity: "[Thoreau's axe swayed] to and fro with the pulse of the pond ... it had commenced to rise and fall ..." More than this, the Pond appears to embody (or at least to reflect) the divine: "Lying between the earth and the heavens, it partakes of the color of both ... It is earth's eye; looking into which the beholder measures the depth of his own nature ... [It] obtained a patent from heaven to be the only Walden Pond in the world and distiller of celestial dews ... It is the earth's eye; looking into which the beholder measures the depth of his own nature ... A field of water betrays the spirit that is in the air ... It is intermediate in its nature between land and sky."

Clearly this intense description is metaphorical, but I should say in a way that is *suggestive* rather than systematic. The Pond is a meeting place of land and sky, of the physical and the spiritual, of "its Maker" (note the capital) and man, and as such it is a unique portal to the divine. The Pond is also a symbol of the individual consciousness, not apparently connected to other ponds by any "visible inlet nor outlet," and seemingly bottomless. To look into the Pond is to look into one's own soul and there to find Nature's God – the only experience of the divine that Thoreau recognizes.

E. M. Forster's description of the ironically named "Sacred Lake" (a small pond in the English countryside) in *A Room with a View* owes a great deal to this chapter in *Walden*, and Forster's description of it probably sums up better than anything else what Thoreau is saying: "[The pond] had been a call to the blood and to the relaxed will, a passing benediction whose influence did not pass, a holiness, a spell, a momentary chalice for youth."

Questions:
54. Explain what is quite so offensive to Thoreau about the plan to pipe the water of the Pond to Concord.
55. Why does Thoreau compare "That devilish Iron Horse" with the Trojan horse?

"Flint's, or Sandy Pond ... ye disgrace the earth."
Bottom line:
Thoreau describes Flint's Pond, Goose Pond, White Pond and the remaining waters of "my lake country."

Summary:
Thoreau's visits to Flint's Pond and what he saw there are described in detail. In a sudden outburst, Thoreau laments that such natural features are named for men who have no real connection with them: *"Flints' Pond!* Such is the poverty of our nomenclature. What right had the unclean and stupid farmer, whose farm abutted on this sky water, whose shores he has ruthlessly laid bare, to give his name to it? Some skin-flint, who loved better the reflecting surface of a dollar, or a bright cent, in which he could see his own brazen face; who regarded even the wild ducks which settled in it as trespassers; his fingers grown into crooked and horny talons from the long habit of grasping harpy-like; – so it is not named for me. I go not there to see him nor to hear of him; who never *saw* it, who never bathed in it, who never loved it, who never protected it, who never spoke a good word for it, nor thanked God that he had made it."

In the middle of Yellow-Pine Lake, projected what men took to be the top of a pine that grew there before the lake formed. When a farmer attempted to take the pine out of the water, he discovered that the top of the tree had lodged in the lake bottom when the tree had topped over into the water. This was, of course, just the reverse of what everyone had supposed to have happened.

Commentary:
Calling Flint's Pond "our greatest lake and inland sea" is comic hyperbole since this is how the Great Lakes were described. In fact, no other lake approaches Walden in Thoreau's estimation: Flint's Pond is "comparatively shallow, and not remarkably pure," and Goose Pond "of small extent." Only White Pond remains unprofaned by woodcutters, the railroad, and Thoreau's own activities. Thus it is "the most attractive, if not the most beautiful, of all our lakes, the gem of the woods," though it is merely "a lesser twin of Walden."

Thoreau's denunciation of farmers who plunder the land and give their names to features of the landscape which they do not love is extreme. However, the story of the mistaken identification of the Yellow-pine shows how little men are in tune with Nature. Note that in attempting to salvage the tree from the pond, the farmer is motivated by the hope of gain, but he is disappointed: "It was about a foot in diameter at the big end, and he had expected to get a good saw-log, but it was so rotten as to be fit only for fuel, if for that."

In calling for "the "fairest features of the landscape" to be named after "the noblest and worthiest of men," Thoreau strikes a more somber tone, for the Icarian Sea is named for Icarus, who flew too close to the sun and fell to his death. It seems that to Thoreau men may only *aspire* to greatness.

Questions:
56. Why does Thoreau say of the man who gave his name to Flint's Pond: "I respect not his labors"?
57. What undesirable human qualities may be symbolized by Flint's Pond?

58. Explain what you think Thoreau means by the last sentence, "Talk of heaven! Ye disgrace earth."

Chapter Nine: Baker Farm

Bottom line:
Hard work and poverty form a vicious circle.

Summary:
The chapter opens with a description of "the shrines I visited both summer and winter," that is, the various stands of trees in which Thoreau found spiritual beauty.

Caught in a rainstorm as he walked "through Pleasant Meadow, an adjunct of the Baker Farm," Thoreau took shelter in a previously abandoned hut which he now found to be occupied by a poor Irish immigrant, John Field, with his wife and several children. Field is an example of a poor, hard-working man who is destined to remain poor because of the relatively high cost of consumer goods ('stuff') that he thinks that he needs or that he wants (tea, coffee, butter, milk, meat, heavy boots, clothes etc.). The result is that Field "was discontented and wasted his life into the bargain." Thoreau urges Field to live a simple, independent, fulfilling life in the woods which would free him from his employer and his creditors. The Irishman, however, has left his homeland in quest of the American dream and will not give it up.

The rain having stopped, Thoreau made his escape: "[I] ran down the hill toward the reddening west
with the rainbow over my shoulder, and some faint tinkling sounds borne to my ear through the cleansed air, from I know not what quarter, my Good Genius seemed to say, – Go fish and hunt far and wide day by day, – farther and wider, – and rest thee by many brooks and hearth-sides without misgiving." Thoreau is determined to "[e]njoy the land, but own it not." He does not want to be limited to working on the plot of land adjacent to his farm but to be free to roam the earth and "come home from far, from adventures, and perils, and discoveries every day, with new experience and character."

Commentary:
Thoreau equates the spirituality that he finds in Nature with that of the pre-Christian ancients (Druids, Vikings). Here one can see why conventional Christian sects tended to regard Transcendentalism as heresy. The references to the rainbow in the second paragraph are, however, self-mocking. Thoreau makes fun of his own temptation to emulate Noah after the Flood in seeing the rainbow as God's sign that he was "one of the elect" and goes on to give a purely scientific explanation for the rainbow phenomenon which might otherwise "be basis enough for superstition."

Thoreau's description of John Field (the name is significant) allows him to oppose the life-styles of a conventionally poor man, "honest, hard-working, but shiftless," with the self-conscious idealism of "a philosopher." Paradoxically, Field will work hard and stay poor whereas, Thoreau the philosopher argues, if he lived on less, he could do less work and live better. Field is literally tied to his field, working in this small sphere every day and returning home none the wiser for his experience. In contrast, Thoreau asserts: "We should come home from far, from adventures, and perils, and discoveries every day, with new experience and character."

Field is one of those who live "lives of quiet desperation." To say that Thoreau's descriptions of members of the Field family are ungenerous is an understatement – the family is, after all, offering him shelter and refreshment! There is also more than an element of racial (not to say racist) stereotyping in Thoreau's description of these uneducated Irish immigrants. In Thoreau's defense, we may point out that these are not actual people but carefully constructed counterparts of everything that he was trying to achieve by his experiment at Walden. Their cabin is near the Baker Farm, which he once contemplated buying, and so they represent what he *might* have become had he gone through with the purchase: "Enjoy the land, but own it not. Through want of enterprise and faith men are where they are, buying and selling, and spending their lives like serfs."

In the middle of a long deconstruction of Field's failed life-style, Thoreau suddenly restates his credo in the most general terms: "But the only true America is that country where you are at liberty to pursue such a mode of life as may enable you to do without these [consumer items such as tea and coffee], and where the state does not endeavor to compel you to sustain the slavery and war and other superfluous expenses which directly or indirectly result from the use of such things."

Can Thoreau possible have been unaware of how dogmatic, bigoted and lacking in humanity the narrator appears to be in this chapter? Can he have been unaware that, in dismissing individuals as dirty, lazy and shiftless because of their ethnicity, he was linking himself to the views of the most prejudiced men of his generation? I believe (and I hope) that Thoreau is continuing the self-mockery of the second paragraph of the chapter in his description of his encounter with the Fields: Thoreau is presenting the dangers of taking oneself too seriously and becoming a sanctimonious bore.

Questions:
59. What does Thoreau say to John Field about changing his manner of life, and what is the man's reaction? What is his Mrs. Field's reaction? What does Thoreau do after the rainstorm?

Chapter Ten: Higher Laws

"AS I CAME ... the more civilized."
Bottom line:
"[T]he human race, in its gradual improvement ... will leave off eating animals ..."

Summary:

Thoreau speculates on the dual nature of man: part savage and physical ("I caught a glimpse of a
woodchuck stealing across my path, and felt a strange thrill of savage delight, and was strongly tempted to seize and devour him raw; not that I was hungry then, except for that wildness which he represented") and part noble and spiritual ("I found in myself, and still find, an instinct toward a higher, or, as it is named, spiritual life, as do most men"). He recognizes, and values, this duality in his own nature, but knows that instinctual animalism must always be in conflict with the aspiration toward spirituality.

Hunting and fishing are activities that "early introduce us to and detain us in scenery with which otherwise, at that age, we should have little acquaintance." Boys *should* be hunters, but it is an activity they will soon outgrow: "No humane being, past the thoughtless age of boyhood, will wantonly murder any creature, which holds its life by the same tenure that he does." Men are gradually evolving toward a more spiritual, less animal state, just as Thoreau has done as he grew up.

Though men commonly think that the time they spend fishing is wasted "unless they got a long string of fish, though they had the opportunity of seeing the pond all the while," Thoreau now finds himself past "the hunter stage of development." He feels that there is something unclean in catching, preparing, and eating fish, and the food itself seems not "to have fed me essentially"; it is "insignificant and unnecessary." Meat, wine, tea, and coffee appeal to man's lower nature.

The food we eat should be consistent with our pursuit of the highest ideals of life: "It is hard to provide and cook so simple and clean a diet as will not offend the imagination; but this, I think, is to be fed when we feed the body; they should both sit down at the same table. Yet perhaps this may be done. The fruits eaten temperately need not make us ashamed of our appetites, nor interrupt the worthiest pursuits ... It may be vain to ask why the imagination will not be reconciled to flesh and fat. I am satisfied that it is not. Is it not a reproach that man is a carnivorous animal? True, he can and does live, in a great measure, by preying on other animals; but this is a miserable way, – as any one who will go to snaring rabbits, or slaughtering lambs, may learn, – and he will be regarded as a benefactor of his race who shall teach man to confine himself to a more innocent and wholesome diet."

Commentary:

The argument in this chapter is convoluted and (frankly) contradictory. Thoreau makes a distinction between love of the wild and love of the good. As an animal, he has often felt (and still feels) the excitement of the hunt for it brings the hunter close to Nature. Thus, he recommends that parents should *make* their sons hunters [nothing is said of daughters!] "remembering that it was one of the best parts of my education." However, just as the individual feels some "instinct towards a higher, or, as it is named, spiritual life," so does the race gradually progress beyond the eating of flesh to a simpler, more wholesome, diet. Thoreau uses the extended metaphor of the caterpillar metamorphosing into the butterfly to illustrate his point: "The gross feeder is a man in the larva state; and there are whole nations in that condition, nations without fancy or imagination, whose vast abdomens betray them."

"Fishermen, hunters, woodchoppers, and others, spending their lives in the fields and woods, in a peculiar sense a part of Nature themselves, are often in a more favorable mood for observing her, in the intervals of their pursuits, than philosophers or poets even, who approach her with expectation. She is not afraid to exhibit herself to them." However, if these men place a value on their time in Nature simply in terms of what they produce, then they miss the whole point of the experience.

Questions:

60. Thoreau argues (with tongue firmly in cheek) that "perhaps the hunter is the greatest friend of the animals hunted." How does he justify this paradoxical assertion? Why does he add: "not excepting the Humane Society"?

"If one listens ... ever increasing respect."
Bottom line:

Man is a sensual being, but sensuality detracts from the purity of our higher nature and principles: "All sensuality is one, though it takes many forms; all purity is one."

Summary:

Humans are dominated by their appetites. When we eat and drink for some reason other than to "sustain our animal, or inspire our spiritual life," then "We are conscious of an animal in us, which awakens in proportion as our higher nature slumbers." In contrast, a life of "purity" (Thoreau also uses the word "chastity"), brings us closer to God: "Man flows at once to God when the channel of purity is open. By turns our purity inspires and our impurity casts us down. He is blessed who is assured that the animal is dying out in him day by day, and the divine being established. Perhaps there is none but has cause for shame on account of the inferior and brutish nature to which he is allied."

"Nature is hard to be overcome, but she must be overcome ... Every man is the builder of a temple, called his body, to the god he worships, after a style purely his own, nor can he get off by hammering marble instead. We are all sculptors and painters, and our material is our own flesh and blood and bones. Any nobleness begins at once to refine a man's features, any meanness or sensuality to imbrute them."

Commentary:

This section represents Thoreau's prose at its most abstract and 'difficult.' The modern reader finds it hard to imagine how a cup of warm coffee can dash the hopes of the morning. Thoreau is making very precise distinctions here: it is not actually *what* one eats or drinks but *why* one eats or drinks. He is not advocating starving the body, since man only lives through the body, but he is advocating nutrition as a *means to an end* (greater spirituality) not as an end in itself: "Not that food which entereth into the mouth defileth a man, but the appetite with which it is eaten."

Coming across the statement, "Nature is hard to be overcome, but she must be overcome," is something of a shock. Did not Thoreau go to the woods to commune with Nature? There is, in fact, no absolute contradiction here. Thoreau knows that everything in Nature (every species and every individual) is *in the process of evolving* to a higher level. We must not (like the Canadian woodchopper) allow ourselves to become 'stuck' in the low level of consciousness that Nature appeared to place us. Nature is, of course, physical, but it is also patterns, laws and truths which we can strive to understand: "Who knows what sort of life would result if we attained to purity? ... Man flows at once to God when the channel of purity is open." It is the purely physical aspect of Nature that man must overcome.

John Farmer, as the name makes clear, is an allegorical figure. If John Field represented those who closed their minds to Thoreau's message in *Walden*, John Farmer represents those who still have minds open to Thoreau's ideas, open to evolving beyond their physical to their spiritual nature.

Questions:

61. How would you describe the role that Thoreau thinks sex should play in a person's life?

62. Thoreau describes John Farmer suddenly hearing a flute in the evening. Who is playing the flute? What does the music symbolize? What effect does the sound have upon him?

Chapter Eleven: Brute Neighbors

Bottom line:

Thoreau observes profound similarities between the animals that he observes and humans.

Summary:

The chapter opens with a dialogue between Philosopher and Poet: the philosopher in Thoreau wanted to complete his meditation convinced that he was "as near being resolved into the essence of things as ever I was in my life," but the Poet in Thoreau was hungry and wanted to go fishing. The Poet won. (We might equally see this dialogue as between two different people: the Thoreau of the last two chapters and a more practical friend who celebrates things as they *are* not as they *might be*.

The remainder of the chapter comprises Thoreau's precise observations of the animals he encountered on and around Walden Pond: mice, birds, ants, cats, water fowl, etc. He observes their strategies to protect their young, their battles [Of a 'war' between black and red ants he comments: "There was not one hireling there. I have no doubt that it was a principle they fought for, as much as our ancestors, and not to avoid a three-penny tax on their tea; and the results of this battle will be as important and memorable to those whom it concerns as those of the battle of Bunker Hill, at least."], and what appears to him to be their simple love of being in Nature: "I thought they [ducks] had gone off thither long since, they would settle down by a slanting flight of a quarter of a mile on to a distant part which was left free; but what beside safety they got by sailing in the middle of Walden I do not know, unless they love its water for the same reason that I do."

Commentary:

In many ways, this chapter is a welcome corrective to the 'holier than thou' tone of the previous two chapters. Here, once again with humor, Thoreau is prepared to acknowledge his own shortcomings and failures.

The opening dialogue between Philosopher and Poet is a reprise of the theme of man's dual nature: the Philosopher representing man's spiritual side and the Poet man's origin as a creature in Nature ("nature, red in tooth and claw" as the poet Tennyson wrote).

The title of the chapter title leads the reader to anticipate that in it Thoreau will describe his human neighbors and criticize them for being so anti-intellectual and unspiritual. Thoreau has thus set a trap for us. The chapter begins with a dialogue between an unidentified Hermit and a Poet in which it is the Hermit who is presented as ridiculous since he gets distracted from philosophical questions by the Poet's more down-to-earth desire to go fishing (a form of 'hunting' that Thoreau has earlier claimed to have virtually given up). Perhaps the dialogue describes two conflicting sides of Thoreau's own character, or perhaps the Poet is his close friend Ellery Channing: either way, the serious thinker in Thoreau comes off worst!

The remainder of the chapter describes not his human but his animal neighbors. Thoreau's descriptions focus on animals involved in practical matters of survival, especially the search for food. Since these animals are, like man, simply parts of Nature, it is not surprising that Thoreau finds many parallels between them and mankind. The behavior of most of the creatures he describes, Thoreau can understand, but the chapter ends with three puzzles: the 'winged' cat, the loon, and the ducks. Each one exposes the limitations of man's understanding of Nature. Thoreau concludes of the latter: "what beside safety they got by sailing in the middle of Walden I do not know, unless they love its water for the same reason that I do." If the loon, "so perfect is this instinct," is taken to embody those higher spiritual qualities that Thoreau strives to attain, then his failure to "discover" the bird when it dove into the water of the Pond signifies how far he is from developing those qualities in himself.

Although it is not so obvious to modern readers, Thoreau's detailed description of the battle of the ants is deliberate parody of the tendency for parable-making (i.e., the drawing of moral lessons from natural phenomena) which "had become during the past century a literary pastime" (Cavell 21). The ants are another sign that man must move beyond Nature.

Questions:
63. Explain the difference in the outlooks on life of the Hermit and the Philosopher.
64. Concluding his description of the battle of the red and black ants, Thoreau adds: "The battle which I witnessed took place in the Presidency of Polk, five years before the passage of Webster's Fugitive-Slave Bill." What point is he making here?

Chapter Twelve: House-Warming

"IN OCTOBER ... had left."

Bottom line:

Surrounded in autumn by Nature's bounty, Thoreau complains about the way commercial agriculture destroys the environment.

Summary:

Thoreau contrasts naturally growing berries and vegetables with those harvested and grown by man. Whilst he frequently left cranberries unpicked (taking only what he needed for himself), the farmers pick them by the bushel. He notes that native plants which once grew in the wild (such as the ground-nut) are being driven into extinction by more quick-growing grains imported by Europeans.

Thoreau is reluctant to abandon his outdoor life despite the falling temperatures: "[B]efore I finally went into winter quarters in November, I used to resort to the north-east side of Walden, which the sun, reflected from the pitch-pine woods and the stony shore, made the fire-side of the pond; it is so much pleasanter and wholesomer to be warmed by the sun while you can be, than by an artificial fire. I thus warmed myself by the still glowing embers which the summer, like a departed hunter, had left."

Commentary:

The title of the chapter is a joke: one normally has a house-warming as soon as a house is completed. All of the owner's friends and neighbors come round for a party. Thoreau's house-warming is different: it involves him generating heat from within so that he can hibernate as do many animals. Effectively, he will be discouraging all but the most determined visitors.

Obviously, winter will change Thoreau's relationship with Nature. Whereas up until now he has experienced the spring of rebirth and the summer and autumn of fruition, under the influence of which he has been renewed and vitalized, now he will be to some extent cut off from Nature and what little he will see will suggest death rather than life. For several months, Thoreau will be forced to find his inspiration from within himself: what his fire does for the cabin, Thoreau's spirituality must do for him.

Questions:

65. With particular reference to the use of language, describe the tone of Thoreau's statement: "I admired, though I did not gather, the cranberries, small waxen gems, pendants of the meadow grass, pearly and red, which the farmer *plucks* with an *ugly* rake, leaving the smooth meadow in a *snarl*, *heedlessly* measuring them *by the bushel and the dollar only*, and sells the *spoils* of the meads to Boston and New York; destined to be jammed, to satisfy the tastes of

lovers of Nature there. So butchers *rake* the tongues of bison out of the prairie grass, regardless of the *torn and drooping* plant" (emphasis added).

"When I came ... to do so."
Bottom Line:
The on-set of winter means that Thoreau has to weather-proof his cabin.

Summary:
It now being November, Thoreau describes building a fireplace and chimney and plastering his walls to fill in the gaps. Paradoxically, Thoreau notes that the more comfortable and convenient his house became, the less pleased with it was he: "My house never pleased my eye so much after it was plastered, though I was obliged to confess that it was more comfortable. Should not every apartment in which man dwells be lofty enough to create some obscurity over-head, where flickering shadows may play at evening about the rafters? These forms are more agreeable to the fancy and imagination than fresco paintings or other the most expensive furniture." In plastering the walls, he sacrificed the natural aspect of wood for artificial plaster. Once again, he found himself caught in the conflict between living an entirely natural life and meeting the physical needs (in this case for warmth) that he had.

He says the same of introducing a stove to replace the open fire: "The next winter I used a small cooking-stove for economy, since I did not own the forest; but it did not keep fire so well as the open fire-place. Cooking was then, for the most part, no longer a poetic, but merely a chemic [i.e., chemical] process. It will soon be forgotten, in these days of stoves, that we used to roast potatoes in the ashes, after the Indian fashion. The stove not only took up room and scented the house, but it concealed the fire, and I felt as if I had lost a companion." Nevertheless, Thoreau records that he got great pleasure in learning the skills necessary to winter-proof his house and enjoyed the manual labor involved.

Commentary:
With the coming of the cold weather, Thoreau's relationship with his environment changed: "I now first began to inhabit my house, I may say, when I began to use it for warmth as well as shelter." This leads to some reflections on the nature of houses. Thoreau imagines his ideal house, a huge, single room dwelling "standing in a golden age" within which many people would live communally. He contrasts this vision with the segmentation of modern houses: "where to be a guest is to be presented with the freedom of the house, and not to be carefully excluded from seven eighths of it, shut up in a particular cell, and told to make yourself at home there, – in solitary confinement. Nowadays the host does not admit you to *his* hearth, but has got the mason to build one for yourself somewhere in his alley, and hospitality is the art of *keeping* you at the greatest distance."

Thoreau's chimney, and the fire which burns within it, are metaphors for man's soul: "the chimney is to some extent an independent structure, standing on the ground and rising through the house to the heavens; even after the house is burned it still stands sometimes." The soul is the immortal part of a man which will survive the destruction of the body. This is why he writes of christening his "new hearth." Nowhere in the book does Thoreau clarify what he means by man's immortal soul, or spirit, but it is this that will see him through the winter.

Questions:
66. Explain exactly how Thoreau feels that the design of modern houses impacts negatively on the lives of those who inhabit them.

"The pond had ... wood fire talked.'"
Bottom Line:
Thoreau describes himself studying and living in harmony with Nature: "I withdrew yet farther into my shell, and endeavored to keep a bright fire both within my house and within my breast." This is the season of hibernation.

Summary:
Thoreau uses the formation of ice on Walden Pond to study the deep waters beneath. He is particularly interested in the air bubbles that form in the ice. He understands how the bubbles act like a lens to magnify the warmth of the sun making the ice "crack and whoop."

In winter, Thoreau is dependent on wood to heat his cabin. This he gets not by cutting down trees but by digging up stumps from his field, by salvaging fallen timber from the Pond and from a ruined old fence, and by picking up fallen "fagots and waste wood" from the forest floor. Not only is the foraging for wood itself a pleasant activity, but it is one that enhances all aspects of life: "How much more interesting an event is that man's supper who has just been forth in the snow to hunt, nay, you might say, steal, the fuel to cook it with! His bread and meat are sweet."

For all his closeness to Nature, Thoreau again acknowledges that humans are different from animals: "Some of my friends spoke as if I was coming to the woods on purpose to freeze myself. The animal merely makes a bed, which he warms with his body in a sheltered place; but man, having discovered fire, boxes up some air in a spacious apartment, and warms that, instead of robbing himself, makes that his bed, in which he can move about divested of more cumbrous clothing, maintain a kind of summer in the midst of winter, and by means of windows even admit the light, and with a lamp lengthen out the day. Thus he goes a step or two beyond instinct, and saves a little time for the fine arts."

Commentary:
The minute descriptions (e.g., of the formation of bubbles in the ice on the Pond) recreate for the reader the higher consciousness which is available to all

once they give themselves time to become a part of Nature. More than this, however, the Pond symbolizes Thoreau himself, each shut off from obvious external sources; the author's study and surveying of the Pond, his coming to know its secrets and to separate truth from myth and rumor, symbolize his process of exploring his own psyche and coming to know himself.

Thoreau's presentation of himself as a model of how to live without damaging the landscape is undercut by his own self-deprecating humor. He is only mock-serious in describing himself as "Lord Warden" of the forests. Immediately afterwards, he reminds his readers of the incident years earlier where he burned down a substantial portion of the forest: "if any part was burned, though I burned it myself by accident, I grieved with a grief that lasted longer and was more inconsolable than that of the proprietors; nay, I grieved when it was cut down by the proprietors themselves." Similarly, he records that one day he came very close to burning down his own cabin.

Questions:
67. Explain how Thoreau feels that "the human race may be at last destroyed."
68. What are the advantages and what are the disadvantages of the way in which man has lengthened out the natural day by creating artificial light and warmth within his house?

Chapter Thirteen: Former Inhabitants; and Winter Visitors

"I WEATHERED SOME ... myself asleep."

Bottom line:

The human life-span is short and human attempts to build dwellings and to store up material possessions are ultimately valueless.

Summary:

In the winter, Thoreau has few visitors and spends the time conjuring up in his memory those who formerly lived in the area of his cabin. Thoreau recalls that, though the forests have been replaced by open fields and the roads are much wider, a generation ago it was more populated than it is now: "Within the memory of many of my townsmen the road near which my house stands resounded with the laugh and gossip of inhabitants, and the woods which border it were notched and dotted here and there with their little gardens and dwellings, though it was then much more shut in by the forest than now." He gives a brief history of those who lived in the area (slaves and freemen, black and white) and what happened to their cabins once they died, for the one thing they all have in common is that they are now in Concord graveyard; each one "occupies an equally narrow house at present."

Though there is little evidence of their houses remaining, the plants which these people planted are still flourishing: " Now only a dent in the earth marks the site of these dwellings, with buried cellar stones, and strawberries, raspberries, thimble-berries, hazel-bushes, and sumachs [related to the cashew nut] growing in the sunny sward there; some pitch-pine or gnarled oak occupies what was the chimney nook, and a sweet-scented black-birch, perhaps, waves where the door-stone was ... Still grows the vivacious lilac a generation after the door and lintel and the sill are gone, unfolding its sweet-scented flowers each spring, to be plucked by the musing traveller; planted and tended once by children's hands, in front-yard plots, – now standing by wall-sides in retired pastures, and giving place to new-rising forests; – the last of that stirp [i.e., line of inheritance], sole survivor of that family. Little did the dusky children think that the puny slip with its two eyes only, which they stuck in the ground in the shadow of the house and daily watered, would root itself so, and outlive them and house itself in the rear that shaded it, and grown man's garden and orchard, and tell their story faintly to the lone wanderer a half century after they had grown up and died, – blossoming as fair, and smelling as sweet, as in that first spring. I mark its still tender, civil, cheerful, lilac colors."

Commentary:

Winter is a time when Nature gives Thoreau little in the way of stimulation; Nature seems dead and "even the hooting of the owl was hushed." Naturally then, the theme of human mortality pervades this section. Each of the individuals named had a life and sought to establish roots in the soil, but their efforts were thwarted by time. All that is left are the disused cellars and the wells of their habitations. Throughout the book, wells (the Pond is "a clear and deep green well") represent the life of the spirit and though the inhabitants are dead, their wells still offer the potential to nourish and inspire others.

Thoreau takes satisfaction from having constructed his cabin on virgin land: "I am not aware that any man has ever built on the spot which I occupy. Deliver me from a city built on the site of a more ancient city, whose materials are ruins, whose gardens cemeteries. The soil is blanched and accursed there, and before that becomes necessary the earth itself will be destroyed." He forgets, however, that he used materials from a derelict cabin.

Questions:
69. Why do you think that Thoreau gives such prominence to the black former inhabitants of the now-vanished village?
70. Select and explain two details of Thoreau's description that bring home to you the fleeting nature of human life.

"At this season ... from the town."
Bottom Line:
Thoreau describes his few human winter visitors.

Summary:
Even winter does not keep Thoreau inside: "no weather interfered fatally with my walks, or rather my going abroad, for I frequently tramped eight or ten miles through the deepest snow to keep an appointment with a beech-tree, or a yellow-birch, or an old acquaintance among the pines." Even now he finds signs of life, like the owl which, when Thoreau approached too close, "launched himself off, and flapped through the pines, spreading his wings to unexpected breadth."

His human friends are limited to an occasional woodchopper, and his friends the poet [William Ellery Channing], the philosopher [Amos Bronson Alcott] and the "Old Immortal" [Ralph Waldo Emerson]. Of the latter, Thoreau writes: "There we worked, revising mythology, rounding a fable here and there, and building castles in the air for which earth offered no worthy foundation. Great Looker! Great Expecter! to converse with whom was a New England Night's Entertainment. Ah! such discourse we had, hermit and philosopher, and the old settler I have spoken of, – we three, – it expanded and racked my little house ..."

Commentary:
Thoreau has spent so much time attacking the fallacies of contemporary thought that it is appropriate for him to here provide a eulogy on thought which *is in tune with* Nature as opposed to being in opposition to it. In a chapter devoted to human mortality, Emerson seems to be the one true exception: his visits heighten the narrator's spiritual awareness. It is in our ideas that we can achieve

immortality not in our buildings. Emerson now appears to perform the function of the Pond by uniting the physical and spiritual worlds: "Whichever way we turned, it seemed that the heavens and the earth had met together, since he enhanced the beauty of the landscape. A blue-robed man, whose fittest roof is the overarching sky which reflects his serenity. I do not see how he can ever die; Nature cannot spare him." Being at one with Nature, man shares in the immortality of Nature.

Questions:

71. Thoreau writes that, in conformity with Hindu philosophy, he keeps regular watch for "the Visitor who never comes." What do you think this means?

Chapter Fourteen: Winter Animals

Bottom line:

Thoreau perceives the unity of Nature.

Summary:

Thoreau relates his observations of owls, hares, red squirrels, mice, and various birds. The animals behave in ways that he understands because they are the ways in which humans behave. Thus, of the foxes he comments: "if we take the ages into our account, may there not be a civilization going on among brutes as well as men? They seemed to me to be rudimental, burrowing men, still standing on their defence, awaiting their transformation."

Even the ice is perceived as a human neighbor: "I also heard the whooping of the ice in the pond, my great bed-fellow in that part of Concord, as if it were restless in its bed and would fain turn over, were troubled with flatulency and bad dreams..." This description catches the melancholy of winter.

Commentary:

Thoreau feels entirely at one with Nature which he consistently anthropomorphizes (i.e., writing about a thing or animal as if it were human). Both are going through a time of trial.

Questions:

72. Much of the chapter concentrates on the struggle for survival. Comment on two experiences that Thoreau has which reassure him that Nature is not dead.

Chapter Fifteen: The Pond in Winter

"AFTER A STILL … air of heaven."
Bottom line:
   Even in winter, Thoreau perceives Nature as a life-affirming force.

Summary:
   "After a still winter night I awoke with the impression that some question had been put to me, which
I had been endeavoring in vain to answer in my sleep, as what – how – when – where? But there was dawning Nature, in whom all creatures live, looking in at my broad windows with serene and satisfied face, and no question on *her* lips. I awoke to an answered question, to Nature and daylight. The snow lying deep on the earth dotted with young pines, and the very slope of the hill on which my house is placed, seemed to say, Forward!"

   Thoreau's first task each morning was to collect water for the day by chopping through the ice. He concludes: "Heaven is under our feet as well as over our heads."

   The men fishing on the ice for pickerel using perch as bait are seen as embodiments of Nature: "His life itself passes deeper in Nature than the studies of the naturalist penetrate; himself a subject for the naturalist. The latter raises the moss and bark gently with his knife in search of insects; the former lays open logs to their core with his axe, and moss and bark fly far and wide. He gets his living by barking trees. Such a man has some right to fish, and I love to see Nature carried out in him. The perch swallows the grub-worm, the pickerel swallows the perch, and the fisherman swallows the pickerel; and so all the chinks in the scale of being are filled."

Commentary:
   Thoreau is here much more positive and energetic than in the previous chapter: the "serene and satisfied face of Nature" has not let him down. He goes to the Pond (his source of inspiration from the start), cuts through the ice of winter, and reconnects with the water and with the beautiful life than inhabits it. As previously, his looking into the Pond symbolizes his own self-reflection.

   The naturalist studies Nature as though it were something *other than* himself, something 'out there.' The fishermen, however, with their primitive method, know much more of Nature than does the naturalist because they know their place in Nature. Quite literally, they fit into the food chain.

Questions:
73. Thoreau writes: "Nature puts no question and answers none which we mortals ask." Based on your reading of this section, what do you think he means?

"As I was ... or hill-side."

Bottom line:

We tend to regard Nature as lacking in harmony and laws simply because our knowledge of Nature is so incomplete.

Summary:

Thoreau describes surveying Walden Pond in order to test the common belief that it was bottomless: "While men believe in the infinite some ponds will be thought to be bottomless." He finds that the Pond is, at its deepest point, 102 feet, and moreover that "the line of greatest length intersected the line of greatest breadth *exactly* at the point of greatest depth." He then begins to speculate whether this is a *universal principle* and whether other such rules might be discovered in the configuration of the Pond concluding: "Our notions of law and harmony are commonly confined to those instances which we detect; but the harmony which results from a far greater number of seemingly conflicting, but really concurring, laws, which we have not detected, is still more wonderful. The particular laws are as our points of view, as, to the traveller, a mountain outline varies with every step, and it has an infinite number of profiles, though absolutely but one form. Even when cleft or bored through it is not comprehended in its entireness."

Perhaps, he speculates, the rules which govern the formation of the Pond also govern the formation of the oceans, of mountains, and perhaps also of the human character: "What I have observed of the pond is no less true in ethics. It is the law of average. Such a rule of the two diameters not only guides us toward the sun in the system and the heart in man, but draw lines through the length and breadth of the aggregate of a man's particular daily behaviors and waves of life into his coves and inlets, and where they intersect will be the height or depth of his character."

Commentary:

Many local people believe that Walden Pond is bottomless which Thoreau interprets as their need to find in Nature a symbol of heaven and infinity, but Thoreau measures it at just over one hundred feet. Thoreau meditates on the way people wish to believe in a symbol of the infinite. In contrast, in this matter. Thoreau is a rationalist: he surveys the lake and dispels the myth. In doing so, however, he speculates on a different kind of infinite – the relationship of all things to the laws of Nature, laws which man is yet too ignorant to comprehend.

Questions:

74. In the first paragraph of this section, what jokes does Thoreau make at the expense of those who believe that Walden Pond has no bottom?

Walden by Henry David Thoreau

"While yet it ... heard the names."

Bottom line:

The waters of the world are one water, not because of economic enterprises but because that is the nature of the world.

Summary:

Thoreau describes one hundred ice-cutters descending for sixteen days on the frozen Pond to capture the ice that will cool drinks in June and July, perhaps in New Orleans or Charleston. He uses an extended metaphor describing the workmen as though they are farmers' laborers who "skim the land, as I had done, thinking the soil was deep and had lain fallow long enough. They said that a gentleman farmer, who was behind the scenes, wanted to double his money, which, as I understood, amounted to half a million already; but in order to cover each one of his dollars with another, he took off the only coat, ay, the skin itself, of Walden Pond in the midst of a hard winter."

In contrast to such exploitation of the landscape, which can transport Walden water to distant regions for trivial purposes, Thoreau feels instinctively united by the water of Walden Pond with the sacred water of the River Ganges. Unable in the mornings to bathe in the Pond, instead he bathes his "intellect in the stupendous and cosmogonal philosophy of the Bhagvat Geeta [Hindu scripture]." In this, he feels himself to be doing the same as did "the servant of the Bramin," and thus that he has integrated Oriental and Western philosophy and spirituality: "The pure Walden water is mingled with the sacred water of the Ganges."

Commentary:

Given the criticism Thoreau earlier made of conventional agricultural practices, it is only to be expected that he should find the 'harvesting' of ice to be another abuse of Nature. He begins by mocking the Concord citizen who, in January, comes to the Pond to get the ice that will cool his drinks in July: "While yet it is cold January, and snow and ice are thick and solid, the prudent landlord comes from the village to get ice to cool his summer drink; impressively, even pathetically wise, to foresee the heat and thirst of July now in January, – wearing a thick coat and mittens! when so many things are not provided for. It may be that he lays up no treasures in this world which will cool his summer drink in the next." Thoreau's point is that this man has got his priorities all wrong: there are so many more important needs to fulfill, and more spiritual goals to attain, than providing ice for drinks next summer.

When the ice-cutters first appear, Thoreau pretends, for comic effect, to a naiveté that he is very far from having. He says that he cannot understand what they are doing: they seem to him like farmers, perhaps "come to sow a crop of winter rye, or some other kind of grain recently introduced from Iceland." (Grain does not grow in Iceland!) He continues to make fun of their enterprise noting: "They calculated that not twenty-five per cent. of this would reach its destination, and that two or three per cent. would be wasted in the cars." It all sounds wasteful and inefficient!

Questions:

75. Fortunately, whilst making fun of the ice-cutters, Thoreau remembers not to take himself too seriously. Explain the joke in his observation: "These ice-cutters are a merry race, full of jest and sport, and when I went among them they were wont to invite me to saw pit-fashion with them, *I standing underneath*" (emphasis added).

76. What symbolic meaning does the ice appear to have for Thoreau?

Chapter Sixteen: Spring

"THE OPENING OF ... in its tube."
Bottom line:

Thoreau takes great delight in watching the thaw of the ice on the Pond which is but one aspect of the green rebirth of nature.

Summary:

Thoreau observes the melting of the ice on Walden Pond as spring comes. He reflects that: "The phenomena of the year take place every day in a pond on a small scale. Every morning, generally speaking, the shallow water is being warmed more rapidly than the deep, though it may not be made so warm after all, and every evening it is being cooled more rapidly until the morning. The day is an epitome of the year. The night is the winter, the morning and evening are the spring and fall, and the noon is the summer. The cracking and booming of the ice indicate a change of temperature."

He then contrasts the sensitivity of the lake with his own (and man's) insensitivity: "The pond does not thunder every evening, and I cannot tell surely when to expect its thundering; but though I may perceive no difference in the weather, it does. Who would have suspected so large and cold and thick-skinned a thing to be so sensitive? Yet it has its law to which it thunders obedience when it should as surely as the buds expand in the spring. The earth is all alive and covered with papillae [small protuberances on parts of bodies or plants]. The largest pond is as sensitive to atmospheric changes as the globule of mercury in its tube."

Commentary:

Thoreau writes about his experience of Nature with an intensity which authors usually reserve for their experience of religion. This is because, for Thoreau, the coming of spring is like the religious concepts of baptism and resurrection: out of death comes new life. It is a spiritual experience. The earth is a living entity, infinite and infinitely sensitive to changes.

Questions:

77. Find and comment upon one example where Thoreau describes the Pond as though it were a plant.

"On attraction in ... of the potter."
Bottom line:

"Thus it seemed that this one hillside illustrated the principle of all the operations of Nature."

Summary:

In this section Thoreau's minute observation of the coming of spring leads him to speculate on parallels between the natural world of the earth and the world of man. Since both are, obviously, aspect of Nature and products of the same Creator, it is only logical that each should embody the same patterns and principles.

He notices and speculates on the patterns created in the sandy railway embankments by the melting water: "I feel as if I were nearer to the vitals of the globe, for this sandy overflow is something such a foliaceous [i.e., leaf-like] mass as the vitals of the animal body. You find thus in the very sands an anticipation of the vegetable leaf. No wonder that the earth expresses itself outwardly in leaves, it so labors with the idea inwardly. The atoms have already learned this law, and are pregnant by it. The overhanging leaf sees here its prototype ... Such are the sources of rivers. In the silicious matter which the water deposits is perhaps the bony system, and in the still finer soil and organic matter the fleshy fibre or cellular tissue. What is man but a mass of thawing clay? ... When the sun withdraws the sand ceases to flow, but in the morning the streams will start once more and branch and branch again into a myriad of others. You here see perchance how blood vessels are formed."

Thoreau perceives the earth as a living entity: "The earth is not a mere fragment of dead history, stratum upon stratum like the leaves of a book, to be studied by geologists and antiquaries chiefly, but living poetry like the leaves of a tree, which precede flowers and fruit, – not a fossil earth, but a living earth; compared with whose great central life all animal and vegetable life is merely parasitic. Its throes will heave our exuviae [i.e., skin cast off or sloughed by a creature or insect] from their graves. You may melt your metals and cast them into the most beautiful moulds you can; they will never excite me like the forms which this molten earth flows out into."

Commentary:

Thoreau perceives patterns in the inanimate sand and clay that are replicated in both vegetable and animal life. This prompts the comparison of man to clay: "What is man but a mass of thawing clay?" Everything is part of the same One, and that One is God.

Questions:

78. What pattern in the exposed railway bank strikes Thoreau most forcibly?

"Ere long ... September 6th, 1847."
Bottom line:

The coming of spring teaches many lessons on how man should live his life. In comparison, literature pales into insignificance: "What at such a time are histories, chronologies, traditions, and all written revelations?"

Summary:

Spring comes with the force of a religious epiphany: "[T]he symbol of perpetual youth, the grass-blade, like a long green ribbon, streams from the sod into the summer, checked indeed by the frost, but anon pushing on again, lifting its spear of last year's hay with the fresh life below. It grows as steadily as the rill oozes out of the ground. It is almost identical with that, for in the growing days of June, when the rills are dry, the grass blades are their channels, and from year to year the herds drink at this perennial green stream, and the mower draws from it betimes their winter supply. So our human life but dies down to its root, and still puts forth its green blade to eternity."

This Thoreau has learned from Nature about how life should be lived: "A single gentle rain makes the grass many shades greener. So our prospects brighten on the influx of better thoughts. We should be blessed if we lived in the present always, and took advantage of every accident that befell us, like the grass which confesses the influence of the slightest dew that falls on it; and did not spend our time in atoning for the neglect of past opportunities, which we call doing our duty. We loiter in winter while it is already spring."

"Our village life would stagnate if it were not for the unexplored forests and meadows which surround it. We need the tonic of wildness, – to wade sometimes in marshes where the bittern and the meadow-hen lurk, and hear the booming of the snipe; to smell the whispering sedge where only some wilder and more solitary fowl builds her nest, and the mink crawls with its belly close to the ground. At the same time that we are earnest to explore and learn all things, we require that all things be mysterious and unexplorable, that land and sea be infinitely wild, unsurveyed and unfathomed by us because unfathomable. We can never have enough of Nature."

Thoreau recalls leaving Walden having lived there for two years.

Commentary:

A major theme of this chapter is *resurrection*: each person has the potential to change his or her values and priorities and to start living in a purer way – each morning is an invitation to do so and each spring shows Nature renewing itself: "Walden was dead but is alive again." In the cycle of the seasons, Thoreau finds a promise of resurrection: if man is mortal, Nature is immortal, and since man is a part of Nature, man partakes in that immortality. This is the truth that Thoreau gets from a communion with Nature that makes all of the written wisdom of men appear trivial and unimportant by comparison.

Spring is likened to absolution: convinced of our own innocence, we are ready to forgive the sins of all men, for in them we see "a savor of holiness groping for expression, blindly and ineffectually perhaps, like a new-born instinct ..." Now, he suggests half-seriously, is the time to open the jails, to dismiss the cases before the courts and to let the church congregations go outside. That we do not do these things is because men "do not obey the hint which God gives them, not accept the pardon which he freely offers to all."

Thoreau has found in Nature the promise of immortality that others (Christians, Muslims, Jews, etc.) find in their holy books. It is not in the concept of an anthropomorphic god that Thoreau finds meaning but in the cycle of the seasons within which his life exists: "Ah! I have penetrated to those meadows on the morning of many a first spring day, jumping from hummock to hummock, from willow root to willow root, when the wild river valley and the woods were bathed in so pure and bright a light as would have waked the dead, if they had been slumbering in their graves, as some suppose. There needs no stronger proof of immortality. All things must live in such a light. O Death, where was thy sting? O Grave, where was thy victory, then?"

Questions:
79. Explain what Thoreau means when he writes, "We loiter in winter while it is already spring."
80. Thoreau describes "a dead horse in the hollow by the path to my house." What rather startling meaning does he take from the presence of this dead animal?

Chapter Seventeen: Conclusion

Bottom line:

"The universe is wider than our views of it." Live your life as you imagine that it *could be*, not in the way that convention dictates that it ought to be; you will achieve a degree of success quite beyond those of your reasonable expectations.

Summary:

Alone amongst the animals in nature, humans set up artificial boundaries to their lives.

Explore the self (not far-distant lands) to understand life's full potential: "What does Africa, – what does the West stand for? Is not our own interior white on the chart? black though it may prove, like the coast, when discovered ... Nay, be a Columbus to whole new continents and worlds within you, opening new channels, not of trade, but of thought. Every man is the lord of a realm beside which the earthly empire of the Czar is but a petty state, a hummock left by the ice ... [T]here are continents and seas in the moral world, to which every man is an isthmus or an inlet, yet unexplored by him, but that it is easier to sail many thousand miles through cold and storm and cannibals, in a government ship, with five hundred men and boys to assist one, than it is to explore the private sea, the Atlantic and Pacific Ocean of one's being alone ... Explore thyself."

Thoreau justifies abandoning his cabin: "I left the woods for as good a reason as I went there. Perhaps it seemed to me that I had several more lives to live, and could not spare any more time for that one. It is remarkable how easily and insensibly we fall into a particular route, and make a beaten track for ourselves." Even living alone, his life had begun to sink into a rut of repetition and convention.

Having defended himself, Thoreau returns to his attacks on the conventional society of his day which breeds the conformity of what we would now call 'the lowest common denominator': "Why level downward to our dullest perception always, and praise that as common sense? The commonest sense is the sense of men asleep, which they express by snoring."

In speaking up for individuality, Thoreau uses the image of the drum that is used to ensure that soldiers march in step: "Why should we be in such desperate haste to succeed, and in such desperate enterprises? If a man does not keep pace with his companions, perhaps it is because he hears a different drummer. Let him step to the music which he hears, however measured or far away."

Fear of poverty is an error that causes men to divert their attention from the things that are important in life: "However mean your life is, meet it and live it; do not shun it and call it hard names. It is not so bad as you are. It looks poorest when you are richest. The fault-finder will find faults even in paradise. Love your life, poor as it is. You may perhaps have some pleasant, thrilling, glorious hours, even in a poor-house. The setting sun is reflected from the windows of the alms-house as brightly as from the rich man's abode; the snow melts before its door as early in the spring. I do not see but a quiet mind may live as contentedly there, and have as cheering thoughts, as in a palace ... Cultivate poverty like a garden herb, like sage. Do not trouble yourself much to get new things, whether clothes or friends. Turn the old; return to them. Things do not change; we change. Sell your clothes and keep your thoughts. God will see that you do not want society."

Thoreau is scornful of society which values meeting important and titled people from distant lands: "I delight to come to my bearings, – not walk in procession with pomp and parade, in a conspicuous place, but to walk even with the Builder of the universe, if I may, – not to live in this restless, nervous, bustling, trivial Nineteenth Century, but stand or sit thoughtfully while it goes by ... Drive a nail home and clinch it so faithfully that you can wake up in the night and think of your work with satisfaction, – a work at which you would not be ashamed to invoke the Muse. So will help you God, and so only. Every nail driven should be as another rivet in the machine of the universe, you carrying on the work."

Almost Thoreau's final vision is of men sleep-walking through life: "We are acquainted with a mere pellicle of the globe on which we live. Most have not delved six feet beneath the surface, nor leaped as many above it. We know not where we are. Beside, we are sound asleep nearly half our time. Yet we esteem ourselves wise, and have an established order on the surface. Truly, we are deep thinkers, we are ambitious spirits!"

Commentary:

Based on his own experiment of living by the Pond, Thoreau appears optimistic about the reader's ability to live a more meaningful and spiritual life. Each person must find his/her way of living mindfully. The final sentences: "Only that day dawns to which we are awake. There is more day to dawn. The sun is but a morning star," show that the book can only be completed by its reader because only the reader can live his own life to the full.

Questions:

81. The story of the traveler riding his horse into the swamp is obviously allegorical. How does it relate to what Thoreau has been saying about man's need to find himself?

Walden by Henry David Thoreau

Post-reading Questions and Activities:

1. Have the massive changes in technology and culture since this book was written made Thoreau's call for people to simplify their lives and give more time to developing a true awareness of the nature of existence more or less urgent?

2. What *might* you do to simplify your own life? Have you any intention of doing it? Why / why not?

3. If you have not seen the movie *Dead Poets Society*, starring Robin Williams, I recommend that you do. Not only is it an excellent movie, but its theme owes a great deal to Thoreau's ideas.

4. As far back as 1984, PBS aired a television program entitled "Affluenza" in which Psychiatry professor Dr. Michael H. Stone discussed "the poverty of the rich." Given what has happened in the decades since this program, what Stone has to say is more relevant than ever. (You should be able to watch the program on the Internet.)

Works Cited / Selected Bibliography:

Cavell, Stanley. *The Senses of 'Walden'*. New York: The Viking Press, 1972. Print.

Dedeo, Carrie-Anne. *'Walden' Study Guide*. GradeSaver. 30 September 2000. Web. 19 May 2016.

McElrath, Joseph R., Jr. *CliffsNotes on 'Walden'*. Web. 19 May 2016

Myerson, Joel. Ed. *The Cambridge Companion to Henry David Thoreau*. Cambridge: Cambridge U.P., 1995. Print.

SparkNotes Editors. *SparkNote on 'Walden'*. SparkNotes.com. SparkNotes LLC. 2003. Web. 16 May 2016.

Stewart, Matthew. *Nature's God: The Heretical Origins of the American Republic*. New York: W. W. Norton & Co., 2015. Print.

Sullivan, Robert. *The Thoreau You Don't Know: What the Prophet of Environmentalism Really Meant*. New York: Collins, 2009. Print.

Van Doran, Mark. *Henry David Thoreau: A Critical Study*. New York: Russell and Russell, 1961. Print.

Appendix 1: Literary Terms

NOTE: A selection of terms relevant to this text.

Allegory / allegorical: a story in which the characters, their actions and the settings represent abstract ideas (often moral ideas) or historical/political events (e.g., *Animal Farm* by George Orwell and *Pilgrim's Progress* by John Bunyan).

Allusion: a passing, brief or indirect reference to a well known person or place, or to something of historical, cultural, literary or political importance.

Ambiguous / ambiguity: when a statement is unclear in meaning – ambiguity may be deliberate or accidental.

Analogy: a comparison which treats two things as identical in one or more specified ways (e.g., "What's in a name? That which we call a rose / By any other word would smell as sweet" [Juliet in *Romeo and Juliet*].

Anaphora: a figure of speech in which a word or group of words occurs at the beginning of successive phrases, clauses, or sentences (e.g. "Some have asked what I got to eat; *if I* did not feel lonesome; *if I* was not afraid; and the like" [*Walden* Thoreau]).

Antithesis: the complete opposite of something (e.g., "Use every man after his *desert*, and who should 'scape *whipping*?" [Hamlet in *Hamlet*]).

Authorial comment: when the writer addresses the reader directly.

Comic hyperbole: deliberately inflated, extravagant language and exaggeration used for comic effect.

Comic Inversion: reversing the normally accepted order of language or of things for comic effect.

Connotation: the ideas, feelings and associations generated by a word or phrase or with an object or animal.

Dark comedy: comedy which has a serious implication – comedy that deals with subjects not usually treated humorously (e.g., death).

Dialogue: a conversation between two or more people in direct speech.

Diction: the writer's choice of particular words (the use of vocabulary) in order to create a particular effect.

Double entendre: a statement that that exploits the ambiguity of language so that it can be interpreted in two different ways - the primary or surface meaning in double entendre is usually straightforward while the second meaning is ironic, risqué (sexually rude) or inappropriate to the context.

Euphemism: a polite word for an ugly truth (e.g., a person is said to be sleeping when they are actually dead).

Fallacy: a misconception resulting from incorrect reasoning.

First person: first person singular is 'I' and plural is 'we'.

Foreshadowing: when a statement or action gives the reader a hint of what is likely to happen later in the narrative.

Genre: the type of literature into which a particular text falls (e.g., drama, poetry, novel).

Hubris: pride – in Greek tragedy it is the hero's belief that he can challenge or even thwart the will of the gods.

Image, imagery: figurative language such as simile, metaphor, personification etc., or a description which conjures up a particularly vivid picture.

Imply / implication: when the text suggests to the reader a meaning which it does not actually state.

Infer/ inference: the reader's act of going beyond what is stated in the text to draw conclusions.

Irony, ironic: a form of humor which undercuts the apparent meaning of a statement (e.g., Cassius is being ironic when he says of Julius Caesar, "'tis true this god did shake" [*Julius Caesar*]).

Juxtaposition: literally putting two things side by side for purposes of comparison and/ or contrast.

Literal: the surface level of meaning that a statement has.

Metaphor / metaphorical: the description of one thing by direct comparison with another (e.g. the coal-black night).

   Extended metaphor: a comparison which is developed at length.

Metonymy: in describing something, a word or a phrase related to that thing is substituted for the name normally given to the thing (e.g., referring to s business man/woman as a 'suit' because that is what such a person normally wears).

Motif: a frequently repeated idea, image or situation in a text.

Narrator / Narrative voice: the voice that the reader hears in the text – not to be confused with the author.

Oxymoron: the juxtaposition of two terms normally thought of as opposite (e.g., the silent scream, black gold).

Parable: a story with a moral lesson (e.g., the Good Samaritan).

Paradox / paradoxical: a statement or situation which appears self-contradictory and therefore absurd but which contains an important element of truth (e.g., "I must be cruel to be kind" [Hamlet in *Hamlet*]).

Personified / personification: a simile or metaphor in which an inanimate object or abstract idea is described by comparison with a human.

Pun: a deliberate play on words where a particular word has two or more meanings both appropriate in some way to what is being said (e.g., "Now is winter of our discontent…made glorious summer by this *son* of York" [*Richard III*])

Rhetoric: any use of language designed to make the expression of ideas more effective (e.g. repetition, imagery, alliteration, etc.).

Sarcasm: stronger than irony – it involves a deliberate attack on a person or idea with the intention of mocking.

Satire, Satiric: the use of comedy to criticize attack, belittle, or humiliate – more extreme than irony.

Setting: the environment in which the narrative (or part of the narrative) takes place.

Simile: a description of one thing by explicit comparison with another (e.g., "My love is like a red, red rose" [Burns]).

    Extended simile: a comparison which is developed at length.

Style: the way in which a writer chooses to express him/ herself. Style is a vital aspect of meaning since how something is expressed can crucially affect what is being written or spoken.

Symbol, symbolic, symbolism, symbolize: a physical object which comes to represent an abstract idea (e.g., the sun may symbolize life or kingship).

Synecdoche: in a description of something, a part of the thing is used to represent or stand for the whole (e.g., 'I see three *sails* on the horizon" instead of, "I see three ships on the horizon").

Themes: important concepts, beliefs and ideas explored and presented in a text.

Third person: third person singular is 'he/ she/ it' and plural is 'they' – authors often write novels in the third person.

Tone: literally the sound of a text – how words sound (either in the mouth of an actor or the head of a reader) can crucially affect meaning/

Appendix 2: Classroom Use of the Study Guide Questions

Although there are both closed and open questions in the Study Guide, very few of them have simple, right or wrong answers. They are designed to encourage in-depth discussion, disagreement, and (eventually) consensus. Above all, they aim to encourage students to go to the text to support their conclusions and interpretations.

I am not so arrogant as to presume to tell teachers how they should use this resource. I used it in the following ways, each of which ensured that students were well prepared for class discussion and presentations.

1. Set a reading assignment for the class and tell everyone to be aware that the questions will be the focus of whole class discussion the next class.

2. Set a reading assignment for the class and allocate particular questions to sections of the class (e.g. if there are four questions, divide the class into four sections, etc.).

In class, form discussion groups containing one person who has prepared each question and allow time for feedback within the groups.

Have feedback to the whole class on each question by picking a group at random to present their answers and to follow up with class discussion.

3. Set a reading assignment for the class, but do not allocate questions.

In class, divide students into groups and allocate to each group one of the questions related to the reading assignment the answer to which they will have to present formally to the class.

Allow time for discussion and preparation.

4. Set a reading assignment for the class, but do not allocate questions.

In class, divide students into groups and allocate to each group one of the questions related to the reading assignment.

Allow time for discussion and preparation.

Now reconfigure the groups so that each group contains at least one person who has prepared each question and allow time for feedback within the groups.

5. Before starting to read the text, allocate specific questions to individuals or pairs. (It is best not to allocate all questions to allow for other approaches and variety. One in three questions or one in four seems about right.) Tell students that they will be leading the class discussion on their question. They will need to start with a brief presentation of the issues and then conduct a question and answer session. After this, they will be expected to present a brief review of the discussion.

6. Having finished the text, arrange the class into groups of 3, 4 or 5. Tell each group to select as many questions from the Study Guide as there are members of the group.

Each individual is responsible for drafting out a written answer to one question, and each answer should be a substantial paragraph.

A Study Guide

Each group as a whole is then responsible for discussing, editing and suggesting improvements to each answer, which is revised by the original writer and brought back to the group for a final proof reading followed by revision.

This seems to work best when the group knows that at least some of the points for the activity will be based on the quality of all of the answers.

Walden by Henry David Thoreau

To the Reader
Ray strives to make his products the best that they can be. If you have any comments or questions about this book *please* contact the author through his email: **moore.ray1@yahoo.com**
Visit his website at **http://www.raymooreauthor.com**
Also by Ray Moore: Most books are available from amazon.com as paperbacks and at most online eBook retailers.

Fiction:
The Lyle Thorne Mysteries: each book features five tales from the Golden Age of Detection:
Investigations of The Reverend Lyle Thorne
Further Investigations of The Reverend Lyle Thorne
Early Investigations of Lyle Thorne
Sanditon Investigations of The Reverend Lyle Thorne
Final Investigations of The Reverend Lyle Thorne

Non-fiction:
The *Critical Introduction series* is written for high school teachers and students and for college undergraduates. Each volume gives an in-depth analysis of a key text:
"The Stranger" by Albert Camus: A Critical Introduction (Revised Second Edition)
"The General Prologue" by Geoffrey Chaucer: A Critical Introduction
"Pride and Prejudice" by Jane Austen: A Critical Introduction
"The Great Gatsby" by F. Scott Fitzgerald: A Critical Introduction
The Text and Critical Introduction series <u>differs</u> from the Critical introduction series as these books contain the original text and in the case of the medieval texts an interlinear translation to aid the understanding of the text. The commentary allows the reader to develop a deeper understanding of the text and themes within the text.
"Sir Gawain and the Green Knight": Text and Critical Introduction
"The General Prologue" by Geoffrey Chaucer: Text and Critical Introduction
"The Wife of Bath's Prologue and Tale" by Geoffrey Chaucer: Text and Critical Introduction
"Heart of Darkness" by Joseph Conrad: Text and Critical Introduction
"The Sign of Four" by Sir Arthur Conan Doyle Text and Critical Introduction
"A Room with a View" By E.M. Forster: Text and Critical Introduction
"Oedipus Rex" by Sophocles: Text and Critical Introduction
"Henry V" by William Shakespeare: Text and Critical Introduction

A Study Guide

Study guides available in print- listed alphabetically by author

* denotes also available as an eBook

"ME and EARL and the Dying GIRL" by Jesse Andrews: A Study Guide

"Wuthering Heights" by Emily Brontë: A Study Guide *

"Jane Eyre" by Charlotte Brontë: A Study Guide *

"The Myth of Sisyphus" and "The Stranger" by Albert Camus: Two Study Guides *

"The Myth of Sisyphus" by Albert Camus: A Study Guide

"The Stranger" by Albert Camus: A Study Guide

"The Awakening" by Kate Chopin: A Study Guide

"The Meursault Investigation" by Kamel Daoud: A Study Guide

"Great Expectations" by Charles Dickens: A Study Guide *

"The Sign of Four" by Sir Arthur Conan Doyle: A Study Guide *

"The Wasteland, Prufrock and Poems" by T.S. Eliot: A Study Guide

"A Room with a View" by E. M. Forster: A Study Guide

"Looking for Alaska" by John Green: A Study Guide

"Paper Towns" by John Green: A Study Guide

"Unbroken" by Laura Hillenbrand: A Study Guide

"The Kite Runner" by Khaled Hosseini: A Study Guide

"A Thousand Splendid Suns" by Khaled Hosseini: A Study Guide

"Go Set a Watchman" by Harper Lee: A Study Guide

"On the Road" by Jack Keruoac: A Study Guide

"The Secret Life of Bees" by Sue Monk Kidd: A Study Guide

"An Inspector Calls" by J.B. Priestley: A Study Guide

"The Catcher in the Rye" by J.D. Salinger: A Study Guide

"Where'd You Go, Bernadette" by Maria Semple: A Study Guide

"Henry V" by William Shakespeare: A Study Guide

"Macbeth" by William Shakespeare: A Study Guide *

"Othello" by William Shakespeare: A Study Guide *

"Antigone" by Sophocles: A Study Guide *

"Oedipus Rex" by Sophocles: A Study Guide

"Cannery Row" by John Steinbeck: A Study Guide

"East of Eden" by John Steinbeck: A Study Guide

"Of Mice and Men" by John Steinbeck: A Study Guide *

"The Goldfinch" by Donna Tartt: A Study Guide

Study Guides available as e-books:

"Heart of Darkness" by Joseph Conrad: A Study Guide

"The Mill on the Floss" by George Eliot: A Study Guide

"Lord of the Flies" by William Golding: A Study Guide

"Catch-22" by Joseph Heller: A Study Guide

"Life of Pi" by Yann Martel: A Study Guide

"Nineteen Eighty-Four" by George Orwell: A Study Guide

Walden by Henry David Thoreau

"Selected Poems" by Sylvia Plath: A Study Guide
"Henry IV Part 2" by William Shakespeare: A Study Guide
"Julius Caesar" by William Shakespeare: A Study Guide
"The Pearl" by John Steinbeck: A Study Guide
"Slaughterhouse-Five" by Kurt Vonnegut: A Study Guide
"The Bridge of San Luis Rey" by Thornton Wilder: A Study Guide

Teacher resources: Ray also publishes many more study guides and other resources for classroom use on the 'Teachers Pay Teachers' website: **http://www.teacherspayteachers.com/Store/Raymond-Moore**

Made in the USA
Coppell, TX
04 October 2021

63470813R00056